Jean A. Miller Mariner

Backward
& Blind

Inspirational Stories
about Teaching Teens

Copyright © 2023 by Jean A. Miller Mariner. All rights reserved.

Thank you for complying with international copyright laws by not scanning, reproducing, or distributing any part of this book in any form without permission, except in the case of brief quotations included in articles and reviews. For information, address Permissions@ CitrinePublishing.com.

This is a work of nonfiction. While these stories are based on true events, some stories depicted here are combinations of several experiences. Further, some events, names, personal characteristics, and qualities have been changed to preserve privacy. All quoted phrases from participants in "The Debate" are paraphrases and not the actual words spoken during the event. The intent of the author is only to offer information of a general nature to help you in your quest for well-being. In the event you use any of the information in the book for yourself, which is your constitutional right, the author and publisher assume no responsibility for your actions.

Cover art by Jean A. Miller Mariner
Author photo by Eliza Jean Mariner

Library of Congress Cataloging-in-Publication Data

Mariner, Jean A. Miller
Backward and Blind: Inspirational Stories about Teaching Teens

p. cm.
Paperback ISBN: 978-1-947708-48-8
Ebook ISBN: 978-1-947708-43-3
Library of Congress Control Number 2023920367

10 9 8 7 6 5 4 3 2 1
First Edition, November 2023

State College, Pennsylvania, U.S.A.
(828) 585 - 7030
Publisher@CitrinePublishing.com
www.CitrinePublishing.com

To all those who participated in my story
as colleagues and students.

I am grateful for the moments of
fun, learning, connection, and humor.

"Jean Miller Mariner is excellent writer whose vivid voice connects so directly and lovingly with students and colleagues who clearly were blessed to share space and time with her."

Peter Thorp, M.Ed.
Educational Consultant to USA and African Secondary Schools,
Retired founding head of school of Gashora Girls Academy, Rwanda

"Any seasoned educator will see elements of their earlier self mirrored back in this memoir. It provides the gift of familiarity and reflection on those first chapters of one's teaching career while also providing a perspective on how far one has traveled in their professional arch. Newer educators will find a sense of affinity and alignment with the rich stories and realities of a fledgling teacher. Regardless of your career stage, you will find this book warm, welcoming, familiar, and joyful. It is a great reminder of the power of the profession and the heart behind why we all do it."

Jessie Barrie, M.A., Ph.D.
Head of School, Bosque School, Albuquerque, New Mexico

"Jean Miller Mariner's *Backward and Blind* distills the wonderful madness of life as an educator into narratives that are at once warm, wild, and insightful. For early career educators, the stories are reminders that the inevitable moments of doubt along the way are often the seeds of lessons that endure long beyond the time students leave the classroom."

Andrew Gorvetzian, M.A.
Faculty Member, Albuquerque Academy

"Here you'll meet an educator who figured out how to educate and inspire her students even during Covid isolation! Her stories inspire teachers, parents, and everyone to be creative, intelligent, and fun-loving, especially in our relationships with teenagers. Prepare to laugh!"

Rev. Judy Myers Hoffhine
Teacher and Pastor

"Jean Miller Mariner perfectly captured the magical interview process, warmth, and love of the little boarding school just east of Pikes Peak. How lucky the school was to have her as a teacher in those early days, and how lucky are we that she captured these moments in these pages!" *Backward and Blind* accurately and beautifully describes the surprises, joys, challenges, and amazing moments that accompany life at boarding school for a young teacher—it's a great read for the aspiring teacher and seasoned professional alike."

Timothy D. Smith
Career Independent School Math Educator, Cate School, Carpinteria, California

"Jean Miller Mariner portrays the experience of the early years of teaching with warmth, humor, and insight. The reader is both captivated by her stories and also understands viscerally why teachers see their work with their adolescent charges as an avocation. So well written and so vivid, this memoir should be issued to every young aspiring educator—they will feel a jolt of recognition and a reminder to stay the course."

Stephanie Lipkowitz, M.A.
Associate Head of School, Albuquerque Academy; Former Advisory Board Member of Columbia University's Klingenstein Center; Founding Contributing Editor to *Klingbrief*, Lead English Teacher and Program Coordinator for the Summer Institute for Early Career Teachers at the Klingenstein Center

"Throughout her impactful career of teaching and learning, Jean Miller Mariner was a keen observer and captivating storyteller. And now we all benefit as she shares her stories. They entertain us, but they also ask us to consider lives well lived in the classroom and in schools, whether we are just starting out or have our own stories to tell. Take pleasure in this book, and then share it with those seeking impact and meaning in their professional lives."

Andrew T. Watson, M.S.
Senior Talent Consultant, DRG Talent, previously Head of School, Albuquerque Academy

Praise for Backward & Blind
Inspirational Stories about Teaching Teens

"*Backward and Blind* provides a masterful gaze into the illusion of being the teacher of children when on a deeper level, the inverse if true. In a look back, Jean A. Miller Mariner discovers the eternal wisdom—just when you think you have something nailed down, you don't. Honest and joyful, she shares through storytelling the lessons a degree can't teach: stay open to the lessons surrounding you."

Andrea Bowen, M.A.
Retired Elementary School Counselor, State of Maine

"This book breaks the standard classroom desktop narrative and shows that teaching is first about connecting with and interacting with humans, both in and outside the classroom, and then secondarily about subject matter. Veteran teacher Jean Miller Mariner does this through relating some epic stories (anonymized of course) that will leave you asking yourself, 'Wow, what would I, as the adult in the room, have done in that situation?' At the same time, she explores reconnecting with her students once they too become adults, further driving home the fact that it's about the human connection. Most of all, you get to peer inside a teacher's personal world of growth as she goes from a young first-time teacher to one who herself has become a grown up in this world."

Troy Lanier, B.E.E., M.A.
St. Stephen's Episcopal School, Austin, Texas; Educator and Author, *Filmmaking for Teens* and *DadLabs Guide to Fatherhood*

Land Acknowledgment

The lush valleys, colorful prairies, hills, and riverbanks that hold the schools in this book are the ancestral homelands and hunting grounds of the Ute, Cheyenne, Arapahoe, Sioux, Pueblo, Comanche, and other first peoples of this land.

Table of Contents

Introduction 13

Part 1: The Choice

Hallway Golf 19
The Former Years 21
This Is the Life 23
Lesson at Dinner 27
The Interview 31

Part 2: Changing Times

Trial by Fire 39
First Comments 45
Date at the ER 49
Cartier Watch and Burgundy 53
Computers 55
The Bright Red Inn 59
It's No Big Deal 61
Words Matter 67
GAFFO to GAFCATS 71
Swim Team 77
The Debate 83

Part 3: Trails and Trials

Backpacking with Jim 91
Fly on the Wall 95
Transformation 97
Grand Canyon 101
Not a Date 105
Leading with Compassion 107
Classy Pregnancy 109

The Great Sit 113
God on Speed Dial 117
Lifelong Learning 119

Part 4: Cruising

Ambition 129
Ancient Mandarin 133
Back at the Salida ER 135
Are We Ever Going to Use This? 139
Ms. Peach 141
Bathroom Break 145
Mouse in the House 147
When You Least Expect It 149
Robert's Theorem 151
Sleepy Time 155
Math Class Is More than Math 159
State Tournament 161
Sounds 163
Navigating Moguls 165
Is It Dinner Time? 169
The Gifts 171

Part 5: The Career that Keeps on Giving

Babies 177
Swimming an Alcatraz Escape 179
Jicama and Headlights 183
Forward and Focused 185
Mrs. Wilmacar 187

Epilogue: Letters 189

Acknowledgments 195
Reading Group Guide 197
About the Author 201
Publisher's Note 203

Introduction

The best deal ever, I think. All I need to do is drive a dozen of my students to Monarch Ski area, and I'll have a free ski pass. This kind of experience is one of the greatest perks of the job and one of the greatest ways to get to know my students. I have to verify they have hats and gloves, and I have to check the medical tent throughout the day to be sure none of my charges has an injury. Otherwise, I am free to ski for the day. With ski passes topping sixty dollars, my six-hundred-dollar monthly income doesn't allow for a lot of skiing on my own dime. I pay for my own ski rentals, but all I can afford are the simple banged up variety that are purely functional.

Mid-February in Colorado provides beautiful skiing with sharp sun rays, crystal blue skies, and dry powdery snow. I am excited and load up the bus at five a.m. to make it to the slopes in time to have everyone skiing by the first run. Bags of bagels sit on the front seat with tubs of cream cheese and plastic knives. These are largely ignored as the teenagers settle in their seats, ready for a two-to-three-hour nap.

Ten minutes into the trip, there is some restlessness.

"Ms. Miller? We need to stop."

"But we just got started, folks. What's the issue?"

"Mark needs to pee," comes a voice from the back, followed by a set of twitters.

My heart sinks. We left town already. There are no more gas stations for at least the next hour.

"Real bad, Ms. M. I forgot to go this morning," Mark is whining.

"You *forgot*?" I shake my head in disbelief and downshift as we ascend through the pass. This is an old bus with a manual transmission: four on the floor, one of which never works. I'm a good driver. For many years, my claim to fame was driving a sixty-six-passenger school bus on Hoover Pass into Breckenridge ski area in a snowstorm.

Other students start twittering. "How do you forget to pee, Mark?"

I look for trees that would suit the purpose with a safe parking area big enough for a bus. The winding road doesn't help his condition. We are not in a section of road where a bus can safely pull over.

"Real bad, Ms. M.," Mark says with urgency.

Eventually, a parking spot near large enough trees and rocks presents itself and a grateful Mark exits the bus swiftly. His "friends" lower the windows and hoot at him as he disappears behind a patch of trees.

With lighter steps, he enters the bus, grinning. "Thanks, guys! Anyone want some lemonade?" Sometimes tenth graders regress to a first-grade mentality.

I maneuver the bus back and forth to make my way out of the tight parking spot. While backing up, I hear (and feel) a singular loud bang. *Crap.* I open the vertical pneumatic doors and slide out of the bucket seat behind the horizontal steering wheel. I walk around the bus, looking for what I hit and the inevitable dent. No dent. No sign of an obstruction. After circumnavigating the bus yet again, I shrug and return to my seat. Then when I back up again, I hear a similar bang. I am quite wide awake now, as are the kids. I repeat the routine, walking around twice, even reclining on the cold sandy parking area to look under the bus with a flashlight—no damage, no obstacle. I step back and look up at the bus windows. Students' faces are plastered to the windows, laughing uproariously. Some are pointing at me.

I pinch the bridge of my nose and look down, sheepishly slinking back into the bus and closing the vertical doors. As I start the bus and we start moving, I hear not only the howling students but repeated bangs as they all start punching the metal walls of the bus interior, making sounds like the bus was impacting rocks, trees, and who knows what else.

I look at my watch. It isn't even six a.m. *Good deal? Ha.* I am working for my ski ticket, and the sun has not yet risen.

Before nine a.m., I purchase thirteen daily ski passes and distribute water bottles. I verify each person has a hat and gloves and is ready to go. By 9:15 a.m., I am on the ski lift, ready for my day.

The first run is magnificent. Monarch grooms its runs beautifully, and I am expecting a great day. As I turn into the base of the ski lift after my inaugural run, I see a note on the chalkboard: "JEAN MILLER TO MEDICAL."

I hobble in my rented ski boots to the tent on the southeast side of the ski area. There is Mark with a clearly broken arm. I'm sure it hurts terribly. The ambulance is ready to load the two of us. I turn in my rented skis and boots, collect his parental medical releases from the bus, and meet the ambulance in the parking lot.

On the way to the emergency room, I ask him how it happened.

"I was challenging myself—" Mark says.

That's not always a bad thing, I think.

He continues, "—by going down a black diamond slope—"

That's okay. I know Mark to be a good skier.

"—with my eyes closed—"

Something clicks. *My skiing day is ruined by Mark skiing a black diamond with his eyes closed?*

Then he continues, "—backward."

I dig deep to continue to be compassionate with Mark as he has his arm x-rayed and bandaged and put into a sling. As I sit on the squeaky Naugahyde chairs in the waiting room of the Salida Hospital, I hold his fancy ski poles and wish I could afford fancy equipment. I have all his expensive ski equipment with me; he didn't trust to leave them unattended at the ski area. I am feeling sorry for myself. I continue to fiddle with the handles of his ski poles and soon discover the tops unscrew. As I open each, I discover they hold a liquid that would do a great job cleaning the bathroom floor. Now I need to alert the hospital staff to Mark's additional health concern.

Mark eventually emerges with his arm in a sling and a sheepish expression. "You don't have to report the gin, do you?" he asks, already knowing the answer. The x-ray reveals a nightstick double fracture in his arm, and his blood test reveals a blood alcohol content just under the legal driving limit. But he is only fifteen and not a legal driver or drinker.

We return to the ski area in time to gather the remaining skiers from their adventures on the slopes. As I drive down the pass to the sounds of heavy breathing with an occasional snore, I contemplate the day. I missed my skiing opportunity and am certainly irritated at Mark. *Backward, blind, and boozed on a black diamond ski slope? Really?*

I consider my own personal adventure into this profession of math teaching, dorm parenting, and swim coaching. Every day it feels as though I am traveling fast downhill in a territory I don't know and for which I have no charts or instructions. Working with teenagers can be as challenging and unpredictable as the moguls on a ski slope. At twenty-three years old, I am contemplating daily how to most effectively transmit information and thinking skills to my students. I am also blind and feel as though I am heading down a hill backward.

It is my hope that I will learn the moguls well enough to navigate them smoothly and wisely, regardless of visibility or orientation; it is my hope that I will not always be traveling backward and blind on a black diamond. It is my greatest hope that I will see risky skier Mark and his bus-banging friends traveling the world with their eyes forward and focused. Each journey starts with a choice. My decision to work with teens as they transition from backward and blind to forward and focused started with taking a job that became a profession that became a life.

Indeed, life itself is a set of moguls to navigate while blind and backward. I would quickly learn that teenagers are not the sole source of moguls in my life.

Part 1:
The Choice

"Choose a job you love, and you never have to work a day in your life."

– Confucius

Twenty-three years old in a respectable research position with colleagues I didn't connect with, I had no passion and no idea what to do with myself. Needing a change, I applied to teach at private boarding schools. I was deemed qualified simply with my college degree. The job seemed fun; I loved dorm life in college. Coaching swimming kept me in the pool, and high-school math was a breeze. I thought I would learn on the job.

As it turned out, I was headed downhill fast during those first years. Teens do the darnedest things at unpredictable times, and the teens in my care were no exception. While the first years were bumpy, I ultimately fell into the career of a lifetime, with wonderful colleagues and energetic and entertaining students.

Why did I think teaching at a residential school seemed fun? It was natural and obvious. After all, both my parents were teachers.

As a twenty-year-old, I felt proud to remember every teacher who stood at the front of my classrooms—that perhaps should have been a brightly colored flag for me. Now in retirement, I can still name every one of my classroom teachers. Further, I can tell stories about them. Thus, the process of this profession choosing me was planted when I was in kindergarten but took over twenty years to flower.

Hallway Golf

1978

It was my junior year in high school U.S. History. I chewed on my pencil and wrapped my ankles around the legs of my chair. Mr. Mulligan instructed us to open our texts.

"Read the next chapter quietly at your seats."

Then he left the room.

We started chatting; no one read the chapter. Hey, we were teenagers. Someone did her nails while others chatted about the upcoming prom. The football players recounted the last successful game. Someone pulled out her art project and began painting. I started on my math homework, thinking it would be good to get it done so I wouldn't have to carry my book home. Someone got up to use the restroom but stopped at the door and beckoned us all to have a look.

In the hallway, Mr. Mulligan's back faced us, in mid-swing of his golf club. He tapped the small ball into a box that reversed the direction of the ball, sending it back to him. He repositioned the ball with his foot, then took another swing.

Mr. Mulligan was playing golf in the hallway during our U.S. History class.

Every Friday Mr. Mulligan gave a ten-question true-false quiz on the reading we were to do while he was playing hallway golf. We decided to divide up the school year—each person would take responsibility for one of the weeks' readings. That person would then, during the test, put a hand on his or her chin for true and down on the desk for false. We all aced the quiz the first week, and Mr. Mulligan was impressed. We decided we needed to appear realistic in our responses on the quiz. We developed a strategy. Each week different members of the class would "take one for the team" and deviate slightly from the chin/desk directive.

As a result, I graduated from high school with a very weak history background. In college, I was afraid to take history classes because my lack of knowledge would be on public display, and I'd be ripe for humiliation. I was unprepared for college history classes. My choices moving forward were limited.

It is said people choose to teach high school for one of two reasons: they loved high school and want to stay in high school forever, or they hated high school and feel the need to redo the experience to "get it right." I wanted the teaching to be done right; I consciously did not want my own children—or anyone for that matter—to feel limited in their career choices.

I actively held on to the image of Mr. Mulligan playing hallway golf. It motivated me to be inspiring and interesting to my students—so they have doors opened to them, and so they have an experience in high school that includes fun.

The Former Years

1975-1991

Even though a career in education is worthy of respect and admiration, the messages I received as a youth did not support such a career. Voices echoing in my head, up to and including my first four years in the classroom, eventually convinced me to discount any serious interest in making teaching my vocation.

1975: "Why would anyone aspire to be a middle school math teacher?" my friend from middle and high school said in a high voice before laughing, mostly at our awkward eighth-grade algebra teacher.

1986: Proudly slicing bread thinly and precisely to show his family's baking heritage, my boyfriend's father said, "Smart people become bored with teaching," in response to my recent acceptance of my first job teaching high school.

He was a doctor who enjoyed sharing moving and meaningful stories about his lineage of fine bakers. The irony of his statement did not escape me—others may deem baking a boring and arduous task, yet he was respectful of bakers' work and skills. As he looked down over his glasses at the bread before us, I wondered, *Did teaching as a profession not deserve the same honor?*

1986-1991: Armed with thoughts that I would only teach a couple years before I figured out what I really wanted from life, I dove into my first years in the classroom at a boarding school. I knew that committing to teach was also a commitment to a low income and likely meant not having international vacations, nice cars, or fancy homes. I was also holding tight to the thought that I had greater aspirations in life, including a bunch of capital letters after my name. However, after a week teaching, I felt as though I had come home to roost. After four years, I came up for air gasping, horrified my life had been put on hold. At my fifth Oberlin

College reunion, I visited my advisor. "I'm not where I thought I'd be! I thought I'd be getting a Ph.D. or an MBA!"

He responded with wisdom, "Are you happy?"

I began expounding on how I was enjoying these quirky adolescents. They challenged me with their questions and insights. I enjoyed learning new material to present. Falling in love with math was not my original plan. I was thrilled I could coach swimming. I gasped, "I get to do all this fun stuff!" It's clear this profession caught me—hook, line, and sinker.

Then he responded with a simple sentence that has stayed with me ever since, "Then why would you ever change what you are doing?"

Slowly, I began to adjust my goals and realize my greatest aspiration was satisfaction with a career, attained by simply being happy.

This Is the Life

Summary 1984

This is the life, I thought as I sipped coffee, graded papers, and picked at a pastry in the Shiny Earth Coffee Shop in Brattleboro, Vermont.

After my junior year in college, I accepted an intern teaching post at an independent school's summer session. I was feeling confident, competent, and relaxed. Immersed in a wonderful job with students I enjoyed and colleagues I respected, I thought I was the best teacher ever; I had created this amazing project for students to complete. My charges, in singles or pairs, were collecting data after lessons in experimental design and statistics. In the pre-cell phone era, we had arranged a time to meet at the school van after data collecting was complete. As the time approached, I collected my papers, stretched, slipped excessive bills and change under the coffee cup for my patient server, paid my check, and strode out the door.

At the van waiting not-so-patiently for three missing students, the remaining teens joked about where they might be.

"Swimming in the Connecticut River," suggested one student. "Leah would think that's fun. I'm betting she dragged Margo out there for a skinny dip."

"Nah, I think they're hanging out at the Shiny Earth," said another. "Margo's sweet tooth would totally outweigh Leah's energy."

"I'm betting Tim just decided to find a bar and play pool," said a third. "He's always trying to pass for eighteen. And boy, he knows how to have a good time." We kicked at the gravel beside the van. I began to get nervous.

"Maybe they are at the police station," suggested one student with a laugh. I looked at her sharply, and a couple expletives thrust themselves into my mind. I decided to go to the police station to investigate and ask some questions. Not wanting to leave my charges, I asked them to follow me. We all paraded in a line through the small town as shop owners peered from their windows. We reached the police station, discernable by the traditional white spherical lights proclaiming the front door.

I led the group up the brownstone stoop and through the large wooden and frosted-glass door. We all stood in the lobby of the nineteenth century police station. Letting my eyes adjust to the darker interior, my gaze slipped past the front counter. I could see Tim sitting on the cot in one of two cells in the back of the room. He was looking expectantly at me. He had been working solo, collecting his data on the streets, but what happened to land him here? And where were the other two? My heart was in my throat, but he looked fine. I couldn't keep my eyes off him.

There were two officers sitting behind the counter looking from my group to Tim, who was now standing and smiling at us from behind the bars. The man clearly in charge pulled his 250-pound frame skyward, placed his thumbs behind his leather belt, sucked in his gut, and let his shoulder-harnessed handgun protrude slightly.

I was twenty-two and dumbfounded, but I raised up my frame to try to counter his.

"Soliciting," he said simply. "Distributing these." He lifted some cassettes labeled with either Woodstock artists or Bing Crosby songs. The officer continued, "No ID, and this cockamamie story about a psychology class…" Tim sported a scruffy beard and blue jeans in a small town where the officers did not know him. The combination of Woodstock cassettes, beard, jeans, and an easy smile warranted significant concern for the officers.

The man in charge directed his comments to me. "So, his story is true."

Tim's project involved asking people about music preferences and completing a brief questionnaire. He tried talking statistics with the officer to explain his intent, but the man didn't believe Tim and likely contemplated calling the local hospital to see if there was a room available in the psychiatric unit. Instead, Tim was escorted to a cell and was told, "If your story's true, your teacher will be here soon enough."

Tim had been in jail for three hours while I sipped coffee in the Shiny Earth. As the jail door slid open to release Tim, I took the opportunity to ask about the two missing girls.

"They're yours, too?" the officer asked. "They're in the back room responding to questioning." My heart had fallen from my throat to my feet. My head went cold.

Leah and Margo's project was to observe people in a grocery store and to record their product choices relative to shelf location. What had they done? My face paled with horror.

"Oh, no worries," the officer responded, now smiling. "These young women apprehended some shoplifters."

The police were apparently collecting witness statements and giving them kudos for their swift and heroic actions.

On the way back to campus in the van, Tim shared his story and reported how it was to nap in a jail cell. Margo's eyes were big when she described Leah screaming and waving her arms as she blocked the exit from the running shoplifters. All this fit: Tim was mellow, Margo was shy, Leah was big and boisterous. I worried about what the response would be from the school's administration.

Later, I ate my humble pie when I met with my supervising teacher and described the day's events. When working with young people, there's an element of being perpetually out of control; this event is a simple example. I appreciated my mentor's admonition, understanding, and kindness. Sometimes being a little out of control is okay; sometimes it feels bad. But often, those out-of-control moments yield the most learning for everyone.

As I stood to leave, I was highly aware of my youth and inexperience but felt more educated about how I could have dealt with the project and events of the day better. On the way out, I glanced over my shoulder in time to see my mentor looking towards the floor, shaking his head slightly, and wearing a smirk.

As turbulent as the day felt, at least no one broke an arm this time.

Lesson at Dinner

January 1986

Money. My own secretary at the door of my 150-square-foot office. Really cool statistics on the computer. Interesting economic theory. My first job after college was a dream job in an economic think tank and a solid start to my career in economics.

The evening was a special celebratory dinner for our office. The place, the table, the people, and the whole experience were high level. We had our own room in the well-adorned establishment. We sat like a family in straight-back fabric chairs: the boss, Dr. Stone; our administrative assistant, Daisy; the computer consultant, Fred; and me. Our server, Victoria, bustled around us, pouring water, topping off wine glasses, replenishing bread—all in the background so as not to disturb us. There were more forks on the table than you can shake a stick at, more plates than I care to wash or dry, more linen than I ever want to iron, and an unnecessary array of stuff on the table: oils, vinegars, salt, pepper, and crystal doodads meant to hold soiled knives. I was convinced this was Boston's fanciest restaurant.

Dr. Stone and Daisy held themselves as if they were marionettes supported by a single string attached at the tip of the nose. Fred, who must have been a computer genius because Dr. Stone hired him regardless of his large beard and hair in an elastic tie at the nape of his neck, was to my left and trying not to fidget. I felt an instant sibling relationship with him.

In this hyperreality of a meal I could not afford, I was humbled and embarrassed. I spun an imaginary fishing line between my left arm and Fred's right arm while we ate dinner.

The meal ended. We sipped coffee in delicate cups. Chitchat slowed. Then the defining moment occurred—a moment I would replay thousands of times before I understood its true significance.

Victoria was pouring water into Dr. Stone's half-empty glass when Dr. Stone said it: "This would be such a delightful place to eat if it weren't for the help." My jaw and neck fell slack, and Fred put the back of his hand on the side of my leg as we quietly watched Dr. Stone review the check, put a dash through the line above the total meant for a tip, and then rewrite the same number in the line at the very bottom of the paper. I felt like a bucket of ice water fell on my head as I grasped under the table for my purse. Dr. Stone rose, then Daisy as he pulled her chair back like a good "gentleman." They were leaving, marionettes that they were, with their backs to us as I dug through the bottom of my bag for any spare change, coinage, loose bills…I saw Fred quickly pulling his pockets inside out frantically looking for that quarter, perhaps left over from laundry change, as we both focused on balancing our stealth actions with our own personal integrity. My heart pounded. We left a small hill of random copper and silver with a couple crumpled notes stuffed under a plate.

"At least Victoria will know," Fred whispered to me. Then we took long, reluctant strides to follow behind Daisy and Dr. Stone. Our footsteps behind them betrayed our loud thoughts—and our very selves.

The next day at the office, we didn't speak. At my desk covered with piles of seemingly a thousand printouts, notes, and newspaper clippings left by Dr. Stone, I was overwhelmed as I wrote the report for the week. Dr. Stone, always meticulously neat, often with only a single piece of paper on his desk, was at the door looking in at me.

The sides of his mouth were drawn as he spoke. "A disorganized desk is a sign of a disorganized mind."

I allowed our eyes to pierce each other, but I did not let his eyes penetrate my gaze. Barely a moment passed before I spoke, "Then what's an empty desk the sign of?"

In less than two weeks, the large desk covered in papers was no longer mine. I'm not sure it ever was.

When my mind replays the evening described above, I always stand up as Dr. Stone and Daisy remain seated. I always speak in Victoria's defense. I always openly give her the tip. In my mind, I practice standing up and standing tall for her so when the time comes, I will respond in a way that underscores my integrity, my support for others, and my belief that all human beings have value.

Sometimes it takes a negative to define a positive. Sometimes the negative adds clarity to a decision in the making. As chilling as the evening was, it displayed a disconnect in my life and gave me the freedom to consider a new profession—teaching. After all, my previous summer intern position had felt settling, fun, challenging, and full of growth.

The Interview

Spring 1986

A light-pink linen suit with a calf-length pencil skirt. A cream-colored collared blouse. Open-toed pumps. Date book, spiral, pen, and paper. Copies of my resume. Swimsuit, goggles, cap. ("No pool, no deal," I said to myself.) Sturdy shoes for hiking. Dress pants. Hiking pants. Sunglasses. My suitcase filled, I was traveling to an on-site interview at a school in Colorado.

New Englanders are provincial. I traveled west to college, landed in Ohio, and broke a New England tradition. My friend, Lori, from high school went to Colorado and never returned. She even skipped her college commencement ceremony in the east because she said it was more fun to be in Colorado. I was open-minded about where I'd look for teaching jobs—New England or Colorado.

It was forty degrees and raining as I left the Boston airport. When I arrived in Colorado, it was seventy degrees under a cobalt sky.

"You'll recognize me," said Leo on the phone the day before, "because I'm as wide as I am tall and wear a goatee. No one out here but me wears a goatee."

Indeed, as I walked out of baggage claim to the pickup area, I saw him. He accurately described himself, but his description should have included a permanent grin plastered on his mug, white patent-leather shoes, and an argyle-knitted vest. Leaning against a small white convertible Mercedes, he smiled. "Let's go for a spin, shall we? We have a good hour before they'll get nervous about where we are."

In the fifteen minutes to the base of the mountain, Leo began, "We are interviewing you over four days because we want to get to know you. Boarding schools are communities of people; we need to be sure you'll be a good fit. We want the mutual decision to be a good one. I think everyone here is going to love you. I want to show you how magnificent our corner of the world is.

"Oh," he added matter-of-factly, "and I saw the weather report in Boston this morning. Pity about that. I played eighteen rounds of golf this morning." I glanced over and saw his self-satisfied smirk. He was in salesman mode.

At the base of the canyon, he lowered the convertible lid of the sports car. The sun brought a sharp and welcome heat to my shoulders and hair. As Leo nailed the accelerator, I looked up at the crags of rocks, the monoliths, and the tall Ponderosas passing by us. The Mercedes humming, the wind whipping, we swerved right and left to stay on the serpentine dirt road with no guard rail. We stopped on a bend of the road about two thousand feet above the plains and gazed out over the prairie. He gestured right, "Over there's the school," then left, "That's downtown." My eyes felt full of sky and warmth. "Let's get to school now, shall we?"

Even though the prairie looks flat at altitude, as we neared the school, I noticed the rolling hills supporting plants I had never seen. We drove over a gentle, yucca-covered hill and saw a lush green valley nestled just ahead of us.

I inhaled sharply. "The school is an oasis."

"That it is," he replied. "That it is."

We rolled through the center of campus, Leo waving widely to anyone walking across the lush green grass of the school. He stopped at the guest house. "Okay, time to settle in. Dinner is at six p.m. You'll be meeting informally with the math department. Jeans are fine."

Unloading my bag for me, he added, "And we already filled the spot you're applying for. So, really, there is no job opening at the moment."

I froze. *Four days? No job?* "Why am I here?"

"Because we need you. I know Dan will find a job for you, because you will sell yourself." He flashed a grin. "And you're going to love it here."

At night, I settled in. The two-hour time change had me tire early but also wake early. The heavy hand-adzed shutters on the inside of the deep window wells caused a black out in the room, but I rose at five a.m. Colorado time.

Opening the shutters, I saw white-out conditions—snow, lots of it, wind howling. I thought of my open-toed pumps and pink linen suit and realized I did not have appropriate clothing. I lost myself in the deep tub covered with hand-painted Mexican tiles, then wrapped my head in a towel and peered outside again.

It stopped snowing. In fact, the air was clear and still. Snow blanketed the trees and spikey desert plants. The glow from the rising sun colored the mountains to the west with what I soon learned was called "alpenglow." Purple sky, pink mountains, white earth. My shoulders felt light, and my breathing slowed with a new physical reaction to the new day and new vision.

By the time I donned my linen suit and open-toed shoes, my clothing was appropriate. It felt about seventy degrees under a Wedgewood-blue sky. I had nothing to lose, so I headed full throttle forward into a blur of people and activities.

Wendell, a French teacher, took me to a lacrosse game in the corner of an oversized field. "Ever wonder how big a polo field is?" he asked. I wanted to say no, I've never wondered, but then I started thinking about the size of a polo field as my gaze passed over the massive patch of green grass before us.

"How big is a polo field?"

"You're looking at one."

I found myself cheering wildly for Wendell's son in the game.

Later, at a noon interview with David, the Dean of Faculty, I heard about his Music History class. "The school is small enough that we can accommodate special classes like Music History." He paused and looked critically at me. "I saw you have some psychology in your background. Would you be interested in teaching a psychology class?" I could not believe my ears and could not stop smiling.

Interrupting the interview, Leo leaned over my shoulder. In a hushed voice, he said, "We have you teaching a pre-calculus class at one o'clock. Topic is proof by induction. I'll come pick you up here at 12:55."

This was the first I'd heard of this. I couldn't remember anything about proof by induction. I immediately said, "Excuse me," to David, then cornered Leo.

"I'm a first-year teacher. You're not giving me any warning or time to prepare. This is not an appropriate request and is, quite frankly, unfair." I figured, *That's it. No job here for me. I might as well continue to have a good time here until my flight home in three more days.*

I watched the class on induction with Leo sitting by my side, arms folded, leaning way back in a student chair-desk combo. Not previously remembering or knowing what proof by induction is, I was happy to learn from the teacher.

After class, I turned to Leo and caught his eye. "Tom's a brilliant instructor. It was fun to have him teach me induction. He connects with kids so well, and he explained this abstract concept clearly. Did you notice how he drew in the quiet girl on the left?"

Leo just nodded.

In the early afternoon, a tall, lanky, loose-jointed fifty-year-old with a calculator and a yellow banana in his breast pocket found me. He spoke through a bushy red mustache. "I'm Jim. I have a pool key. You and I are swimming at five o'clock." Then he nodded and left.

Turned out, Jim was the boys' swim coach. There was no girls' team.

Jim was a fast and skilled swimmer. I could stay with him for about twenty yards, then the altitude grabbed me. I thought, *I'll be exhaling a complete lobe of my lung soon.*

Between sets he asked, "Ever been camping?"

"No."

"Backpacking?"

"I've climbed Mt. Washington with my dad." Jim reminded me of my dad.

"Willing to try?"

"Sure. I mean, yes." I realized this new place had gifts I had not previously considered.

With one swift, sleek movement, Jim hauled himself out of the pool and into a standing position. "Cocktail party—thirty minutes. Big house on the hill. Can't miss it. See you there." I could tell he was a science teacher by his speech.

I arrived at the party with wet hair, smelling like chlorine, and noticed Jim chatting with the higher-ups. I was handed a strong margarita and was surrounded by a semicircle of doting, twenty-something-year-old, handsome mountain men from schools like Yale, Bowdoin, UVA, and Dartmouth. I looked around and saw a few older women in the company of many more men, but this was clearly a school still in transition from being a boys' school.

Leo took me by the crook of my arm and said, "Jim says you can swim. Can you coach swimming?"

"Yes. But there's no girls' team."

He smiled, "Not yet."

Back in the Mercedes on the way to the airport, I figured, *That's it. It was a fun vacation. I met some great people, had drinks at a party, swam a couple good workouts, watched athletic events, learned some new ideas, and hiked through a desert prairie.*

"Contract will go in the mail this afternoon," said Leo.

Not really believing this, I sat silently.

"When you cheered for Wendell's son—" Leo shook his head slightly. "Wendell wants you to teach his son. He thinks you'd be good." He glanced over at me. "We need a girls' swim coach, and Jim says you're perfect. Dan enjoyed his conversation with you about community. David's been thinking about adding a psych class, too." Leo paused for effect, "You had me when you said you wouldn't teach that class. I need to be sure whoever we hire can stand up to me."

A week later, I was looking out the window of my office in downtown Boston, watching the sleet slide down the plate glass, and holding the unsigned contract in my hand when Leo phoned. "I played eighteen holes of golf this morning."

Part 2:
Changing Times

*"The meaning of life is to find your gift.
The purpose of life is to give it away."*

– Pablo Picasso

Just because you've been in a classroom doesn't mean you know how to run one. You are indeed blind while conducting class, like heading down the moguls of a black diamond ski run. I learned this fact repeatedly over the course of my career. Later in my career during the pandemic, this statement morphed to, "Just because you have been on zoom doesn't mean you know how to run a zoom classroom."

Regardless of your training, the first year is an experiment in survival and simply staying on your feet as you swoosh swiftly down the mountain. The second year is the time to tweak those lesson plans from the first year and remember that mogul you didn't see that caused the fall. The third year is the year to introduce a personal style and personality into the act and performance of teaching.

It is not only the methods and style of instruction that new teachers navigate. Layered on those challenges, teachers need to contend with the changing tides of cultural norms.

During my first years in the classroom, tension grew between traditional boys' school culture and the emerging coed culture that included girls and women. When a school was only for boys, neither students nor staff had to contend with fairness and equality issues, such as dress code, safety, dorm visitation, locker rooms, and so forth. In the emergent coeducational culture, students and staff needed to provide a new atmosphere that included women having their own identity, ideas, skills, and income. The boys' school culture was an outgrowth of a society requiring women to be associated with men to have the benefits of things as simple as a credit card.

I entered a largely male faculty at a school originally intended for boys only, until not too many years earlier. I challenged norms in the predominantly male and often toxic culture, sometimes without knowing it, and sometimes knowing I needed to do something to make the world more livable for myself and others.

Cultural standards shifted widely during my teaching tenure between 1986 and 2021, and they continue to shift. Seeped within my stories of my first years teaching are struggles within the women's movement, depicting the challenge, the frustration, and the creaks and groans as our communities adjusted to a new set of norms.

Trial by Fire

September 1986

With their loud, newly deep voices, scruffy faces, and lanky strides, thirteen energetic fifteen-year-old boys bumped into each other and guffawed loudly as they paraded into the room. They chose seats by putting a hand on the back of a chair, jerking it so the feet scraped loudly on the linoleum floor, and slipped onto the wooden seat. While leaning forward with elbows and arms on the attached desk, or way back so the front feet of the desk rose by eight to twelve inches, each boy surveyed the room adorned with posters of the Golden Rectangle, Pascal's Triangle, and geometric representations of the Pythagorean Theorem. Each then nodded his head and looked at the others with a smirk. One boy, throwing a sideways look my way with a hint of a squint, said, "This will be such a great year."

I was not intimidated, though I should have been. These young men were part of the same athletic team and moved, thought, acted, and responded as one unit.

This was my first day in the classroom. *Does it show?* I wondered. *At least she'll be on my side,* I thought as I looked out at the only young woman who arrived after the Napoleonic youths. She strategically looked at her hands resting on top of each other on her desk.

Raising up my full five feet, four inch and 125-pound frame, I asserted my leadership by taking attendance. "Jack? Henry? Dan? Harvey? Daniel? Gary? Danny? Fred?" *Wow, three versions of Daniel—Dan, Danny, Daniel—can I keep this straight?* Looking up from my neatly printed, brand-new gradebook, I saw their confidence soar.

"My official name is Henry, but I go by Ralph." I took note. *Maybe Ralph is a middle name.*

Fred said, "I go by Binky." I didn't take note.

Gary said, "I go by Goober." I didn't take note of this, either. I felt very savvy to observe their subtle insubordination and not respond. I was above that.

"Jonathan?" Silence. I looked up from my gradebook.

"I go by Jon. Definitely not Jonathan." I took note.

"Topher? Will?" Same last names, so I looked up. Identical twins, dressed alike with the same hairstyle. Each young man faced slightly left with his right foot forward, and each right arm draped singularly on the chairback. Will sported a dimple in his left cheek; Topher did not. I took note. I was checking boxes. I had this "know the kids" thing down.

"Billy? Jake?" And, of course, the fourteenth student, "Cat."

All attention moved to Cat as her classmates reoriented themselves towards her to show their best smiles.

From a reclining position in the chair-desk combo...*How does she do that?*...in the back left of the room, Cat arched her back and stretched like a feline vine, letting her cropped t-shirt ride up and her hair fall back. Surely she sensed the intensity of the twenty-six eyes still barely in the sockets of her classmates, sitting erect with arms hanging limp and knuckles grazing the floor. She slipped off her shoes and pranced around the room swaying beside each young man before she eased into the space between the class and me. I stared in disbelief at this confident and silky approach for a fifteen-year-old in front of thirteen young males. Legs together, gently bending her knees, pertly extending her backside, and holding my stare, she grabbed her crotch deeply and swayed, "I have to pee really bad."

Cat was not "on my side."

All eyes followed her to the door, drinking her in. Jack released a guttural sound, as if beyond his control; his peers chuckled, then progressed to louder heckling aimed at Jack. He grinned widely, loving the attention.

"Classroom policies include—" I began, but no one was listening. Well, maybe Harvey was listening in the back. "Classroom policies include..." I spoke louder, and the boys in the room opened their binders. The interruptions to my course introduction didn't bother me, but I took note.

After I announced, "This course includes a written homework assignment each night of class," Jack asked, "Does that mean we have homework every night?"

After I announced, "Tests occur every other Friday," Jack proclaimed, "My mother says I don't have to take any tests." He was clearly a well-practiced expert in delaying learning and disarming a new teacher.

I glanced down at my notes and continued, "The school's honor code states..." I noticed Jack is now sitting on top of his desk. I stopped and looked at him.

"What?" he asked, trying to appear innocent. "I'm more comfortable here."

I instructed him to sit in the chair, but we had already engaged in low-level battle. I was worried I wouldn't get through everything: integrity, homework, the text, the test and quiz schedule, how to take notes, and office hours.

At least I was off and running; the students other than Jack were subdued.

At the end of the interminable forty-five minutes, the students gathered their new texts, three-ring binders, protractors, and wits into their backpacks and left the room looking as though they just awoke from a long sleep. Jack's classroom supplies remained on, under, and around his desk; he was long gone. I collected his supplies and stored them for him to pick up.

I slipped into the round lunch table with the other faculty members. I was the only woman. I only knew some of the men. The Dean of Students, who made the schedule and assigned students to classes, clearly having shared some stories about me to others at the table, turned to me and asked, "How'd it go?" His smirk assured me he knew about the 13:1 male/female student ratio in my morning class and knew the youths in my room. I wasn't sure how to respond, so I didn't. Teachers universally love to talk, and my new colleagues saved me from answering.

The conversation moved to the philosophy of how to help a first-year teacher best. "I believe in trial by fire," I heard the dean say. "Then we know if the teacher has it in him."

My heart sank. I saw I had a lot of work to do here. First, I was not a "him," and second, I would be experiencing a "trial by fire" my first year in the classroom. I decided to introduce myself to the others at the table and discovered one of the men was the hockey coach.

"Jean has some of your players in class," explained the dean, nodding to the coach, who leaned over his plate to eat and wore a baseball cap.

"How are my athletes doing? Respectful, I hope?" He shifted in his seat, removing an elbow from the table and placing a hand on his hip, elbow out.

"I'm a little concerned," I started, not sure what to say. I described the mild insubordination on the first day. In my inexperience, I didn't consider what his response would be to his players or how his players would respond to hearing I'd spoken with their coach.

Dress for success, I thought the next morning. Looking in my closet at patched jeans, t-shirts, and a singular skirt, I tied a scarf around my neck to look a little more professional with a skirt and a monochrome t-shirt. Holding a coffee mug, I felt somehow professional. In the mirror, I saw a Teacher at the Start of Her Second Day.

Walking with purpose, I started the short distance between my apartment and my classroom. Full of confidence, the leather briefcase my mother gave me in my right hand and a mug in my left, I made my way down the hill to the classroom building. I raised my mug, dipped my head, and lifted a finger to greet colleagues headed in the same direction. *A knowing kinship*, I thought in my naivete and blindness. In truth, they all knew far more than I, and their smiles belied what they suspected was in store for me.

In the hallway, students from other classes waited outside their locked classroom doors. Not so for mine. The empty hallway surrounding my classroom door felt, indeed, foreboding. I knitted my brow with curiosity as I turned the handle of the surprisingly unlocked classroom door.

It was loud and confusing in the room. The boys were rearranging the desks, hiding the real issue—who got to sit next to Cat. They elbowed each other, laughed in low tones, and stood in power poses with crossed arms, spread legs, and slightly arched backs. Several students stood and placed their hands on the desk in front of them, palms down. Cat was the only one not looking at me; she was just finishing giving herself a manicure.

I placed my books and coffee mug on the desk, plastered on my widest grin, leaned against the teacher desk at the front of the room, and prepared to greet them. *Kindness,* I thought. *Kindness always wins.*

Inhaling deeply, I looked out at my charges, mentally organizing myself for the next forty-five minutes. Then Fred sauntered in, swinging his legs widely, letting his feet slap on the linoleum, and grinning ear to ear. "Glad you could join us," I said, trying to minimize my sarcasm and include a tone of discipline.

Fred stopped in his tracks, looked at me with an excess of kindness, and spoke slowly, "Likewise, Ms. Miller. Likewise."

Harvey thought this was very funny and stifled a chuckle. I lowered my head and pinched the bridge of my nose, trying hard not to join the low chuckles filling the air. Fred settled in his chair, still grinning, slouching, having won the interaction.

"How many of you are on the hockey team?" I surveyed the raised hands and realized more than half of the students were athletes on the team. "I met your coach yesterday. He wanted me to report to him daily how you are doing in class. Success in academics is important to him," I smiled.

These few sentences, coupled with my sunny persona, threw fuel on the fire.

Jack stood, simply beside himself. He grabbed a chair-desk combo and slammed it, sending it across the room. He was blind with rage. "You talk with the coach, and he won't let me play."

My heart was beating rapidly; I felt heat on my face.

"Jack, you continue like this, and you'll be out for the season. If you can't control yourself now, then you'll be missing the next week of practice and whatever games are scheduled."

Chastised, he sat. He controlled himself. I felt in control and elevated myself mentally. I started the lesson, simply psyched to start my new career.

"Point, line, plane: the three undefined terms in geometry..." I began.

First Comments

October 1986

After the first six weeks of class, teachers record tentative quarter grades and include a written "comment" about each student. I was proud of my comments; I could turn any negative into a positive to suit our parents. I also recorded short stories in my gradebook so I could share these moments with parents in the notes on report cards. I wrote Ralph's comment:

> Ralph is an energetic young man who sits near the front of the room. Sometimes tardy to class but always enthusiastic about participating, especially when he can present his solution to a homework problem at the board, he keeps class lively. He's not shy or concerned about whether his solution is correct or not. It's refreshing to see such fearlessness in front of peers.
>
> It's clear math is challenging for him, and he reports it's not his favorite subject. Thus, the challenges of completing homework regularly and taking notes in class are very real for him. Without a record of the class lessons, and without adequate practice, Ralph's understanding is compromised as evidenced on his tests and quizzes. For examples, he could not use the Pythagorean Theorem correctly on the last test of the quarter, and during class, he could not correctly identify the triplets we've used repeatedly, even when he had access to his notes. A chemistry problem included in his homework assignment and a couple pages of history notes buried in his math notebook suggest he also has organizational trouble.
>
> Ralph will be participating in a structured study hall program and will meet with me regularly to help him get on the right track

and find greater success in this course. An update of his progress will be sent home at the next comment period.

A polite translation is understood by the experienced comment reader and clear to the parents who know their child:

> Ralph can't sit still and is a disruption in class. He loves being the center of attention and doesn't care if he can do the math correctly or not. He's not skilled at math and does nothing to increase his skills. He has not learned much, so we are putting him in a detention program where we can monitor his homework effort more effectively.

I was surprised when the head of my division called me into her office the morning after I submitted my comments. I could tell by her voice all was not well. I was worried. I didn't even know what I had done wrong.

She started, "You don't seem to know your students very well." I was shocked. I thought I did.

I threw the question back at her, "What makes you say that?"

"For one thing, the student you have with last name Caperton is not 'Ralph.' It's Henry. How did you ever come up with Ralph?"

I was horrified. I checked my notes. In my gradebook, the name Henry was crossed out and "Ralph" was written over it. My brain sailed back to the first day, taking attendance, when Henry said, "I go by Ralph," and I realized I had been the butt of a class joke for over a month. How many times had I called Henry, "Ralph?" Likely dozens.

"Further, Jonathan's mother insists he be called Jonathan. Not Jon. Jonathan is his given name and all official correspondence from the school refers to him as Jonathan."

I was speechless as my boss continued. "Your student Gary prefers to go by "Goober." And Fred is "Binky." If you knew your students, you'd have used the names they prefer. These are the names that would bring you closer to your students. We are an independent boarding school and like to pride ourselves in knowing our students. We like to think each teacher connects deeply and well with the students."

I glanced down at the class list in my open gradebook. I had a vague memory of Gary and Fred both telling me these names and thinking they were just teasing me, setting me up to be part of a class joke. I thought I was so savvy. So on the first day, I had recorded the joke name and not recorded the real ones.

I looked down and blinked, looking at my notes in my gradebook and feeling my cheeks swollen and burning. *Would this get better?* I wondered. *Would I still be making these mistakes in five or ten years?*

In the classroom the next day, I used the corrected names and tried to avoid eye contact with my young and cocky students.

Date at the ER

November 1986

Many a time, the quote from the schoolteacher, Etta Pierce, in *Butch Cassidy and the Sundance Kid*—about being twenty-six, single and a schoolteacher, and hitting the bottom of the pit—painted the picture of my life.

Dates for boarding schoolteachers are rare and sometimes fraught with additional challenges of oddly timed phone calls with unusual requests. Typical meet-and-mingle events were not always possible for us; the struggle was real. Whenever a date would pick me up from my apartment, at least a dozen teenage girls would be peering out their windows—pointing, laughing, giving a thumbs up or a thumbs down, and generally mocking the date. The next week before class started, I always heard about what the girls thought of my date, and I'd either get a nod, as in "Go for it," or I'd get a tilt of the head to the side, as in "Not for you, Ms. M." The faces smearing the glass windows always made an impression and made it difficult to have second dates.

I had dreams of having a life partner, children if we were fortunate, and a shared existence doing things we both loved. Boarding school life made dating a challenge. Was it possible?

My first and most memorable date while a dorm parent was on a Saturday night about seven p.m. I put on my favorite shirt, he arrived on time, and I was just shutting the door to my apartment and asking, "How's Italian?" when my inside line rang. Each faculty member who lived on campus had two phones, each with a distinctive ring—one for school business, the other for personal use. I looked at my date and said, "Mmmm, do I get it? It's my inside line." This really wasn't a question. On the other end of the line was the school nurse speaking quickly.

"There are girls, two or three in your dorm, who I have on the other line. They are in the payphone booth and have eaten a houseplant. I'm sure it's poisonous by their physical reactions. You need to go upstairs, find out who they are because they won't tell me, and take them to the ER immediately."

I shot my date a look of desperation and signaled for him to drive around to the main entrance to the dorm. I ran up the stairs to find the girls.

In the common area, I found Fern and Aria huddled in the payphone booth and the plant—missing some large leaves—hanging in a planter nearby. I ripped the plant from the pot, dark soil spilling onto the carpet as the roots dangled below my clenched fist. With an arm around each girl and a hand clutching the remains of the plant, I escorted them to the backseat of my date's car. He drove while I sat between them, talking with them, holding them as they cried. I guess this was the ultimate test for a date's ability to adjust to any situation.

Between the girls' choking sobs, I came to understand they had been hungry and decided to make a salad from the houseplants in the dorm.

Arriving at the ER, the girls were taken immediately back to the recesses while I handed the houseplants with dangling roots and dirt over the counter to the hospital staff. My heart was racing. I was so worried and simply wired. The two of them were genuinely terrified. The nurse behind the counter asked a set of required questions but needed parental permission to treat the girls, especially as the plant was identified as a philodendron, or rhododendron, or something -dendron, which can crystalize in the kidneys and potentially cause kidney failure. I was handed the desk phone and dialed Fern's parents. Mrs. Rose answered the phone. I was shaking. The conversation did not go well.

"Mrs. Rose?" My voice wobbled. "I'm at the ER with Fern, she has just—" and I couldn't finish the sentence. Connecting Fern's name with "plant" was suddenly very, very funny to me. So, I laughed. My laugh was a hard, uncontrollable belly laugh—from stress and fear and disbelief of what was happening. I handed the phone to the nurse who finished the conversation. I was sure I'd be fired, but I still couldn't stop laughing. The nurse took over for the second conversation with Aria's parents, which was an excellent move. She covered well for me.

My date and I were escorted swiftly into the depths of the ER, where the girls sat clinging to each other. Apparently, it had been too long since they ingested the plant and inducing vomiting with a stomach pump would no longer be effective. The girls needed to drink a charcoal shake immediately. The charcoal would absorb the poison before it entered the bloodstream. The staff asked us to please help the girls drink the thick chalk-mud mixture. My date and I coaxed the girls to drink. "It tastes like chocolate," I tried. But the charcoal also tickled the gag reflex. Neither girl was able to swallow enough of the charcoal shake quickly enough to meet the satisfaction of the ER doc, so it was decided naso-gastric tubes would be used to fill their stomachs with charcoal. I leaned over Fern, keeping her arms tucked by her side and not flailing. My date did the same for Aria. The staff inserted the tubes through their noses into their stomachs. "Swallow!" the nurses yelled at the now crying girls. I was attentive to Fern's flushed face and tears pouring down her cheeks. I glanced up to the table on the other side of the room to see my date being patient with Aria as he calmed her in a soft voice and held her still. Then Fern burped—maybe belched is a better word—and a cocktail of black charcoal, mucous, and blood splashed on my face and favorite shirt. I held her tighter and spoke soothingly through my tight throat.

Then, just as quickly as it had begun, it was over. We all had to wait to see if the girls developed any symptoms. We rested uncomfortably next to Aria and Fern as they tried to rest. They were released at about three a.m. into our custody. I delivered them to the school nurse who would observe them for the next forty-eight hours, looking and testing for signs of kidney failure. We returned to my apartment. My date draped himself on my couch, asking to sleep there for a couple hours. I returned to my bedroom and collapsed into a deep sleep. I was sure to call Mrs. Rose the next morning to explain and to apologize. She was patient and kind, for which I was thankful. The following winter holiday, Mrs. Rose sent me a large and beautiful pine wreath, which helped me understand she genuinely forgave my inappropriate belly laugh.

Aria and Fern were fine. They did not suffer any long-term consequences—other than embarrassment and a good story. But word of their experience spread through the school like wildfire in a hundred-mile-an-hour wind. They were presented with an award at our next All-School Meeting: a flowerpot stuffed with carrots, celery, and broccoli. And while I'm sure they wish this story would fade into the backdrop of their high school experience, these kinds of stories do not die. Thirty-four years have passed. Fern is now a member of the Board of Trustees, where the chair of the board asks her how rhododendrons taste.

And my date? I was impressed with his compassion and ability to adapt to this unique and challenging situation. Certainly, he'd be a great dad. He didn't even seem to mind that we never had dinner or went to a movie; after all, our experience was like a movie, and after a night at the ER, neither of us felt like dinner. I was disappointed when I realized we didn't "click." I'd rather remain single than with someone who didn't flow in the same current as I did. As we drifted apart, I had to wonder if boarding school life was not for everyone. *Was my job creating barriers to finding a life partner?*

Cartier Watch and Burgundy

1986

The brother of a faculty member had found financial success and gifted my colleague a Cartier watch. My colleague wore it discreetly under his starched shirt, enjoying the feel of opulence and the sign of affection from his brother.

One day in class, while reaching up to record something on the blackboard, his sleeve pulled back and revealed the watch. A student born into wealth gasped, "Mr. Rolando! That's a Cartier watch!"

"No, it's not," replied my colleague, with a combination of horror and embarrassment.

"Yes, it is! My dad has one just like it! And you're just a teacher!"

Thinking quickly, Mr. Rolando turned and stooped lightly towards the student, put an index finger to his lips, and spontaneously said, "Shhhh, I'm in the witness protection program."

You could have heard a pin drop in the room.

The students were buzzing after class. Soon the whole school was wondering about Mr. Rolando's past life. A teacher's life is often shrouded in mystery for students. Sometimes students seem amazed we go to the grocery store, use the restroom, or have families. Some students seem to think we live in our classrooms, bidding them farewell every afternoon and pining for them until eight in the morning when we greet them enthusiastically. Mr. Rolando was a genius for feeding a student a line and having the entire student body create a past for him that was full of adventure, guile, bravery, and intrigue.

Often, particularly at private schools, there's a class difference between the student and teacher. Both parties are aware of the differential. It's occasionally the source of great tension when sixteen-year-old students, for example, drive cars valued at five times a teacher's annual salary. However, also most often, students are much less aware of this differential than the faculty members themselves.

Brent was one of those students. He appeared before a disciplinary meeting after being "busted" for drinking wine at the meal before prom, in direct violation of the school's alcohol policy. He was facing possible expulsion. The philosophy of the discipline committee was first and foremost to understand the student's actions and motivations and then to levy an appropriate response.

"So, why, Brent, did you choose to have alcohol with your meal when you knew it was against school policy?" the chair of the disciplinary committee asked.

"But sir, how could I have chateaubriand without burgundy?" the young man scoffed, aghast.

Now it was time for the adults in the room to be silent. We looked blankly at each other until one of us asked what all of us wondered.

"What's chateaubriand?"

Computers

1987

In 1987, we wrote comments for students on typewriters or by hand, correcting errors with white-out on the three different copies—yellow for teacher records, pink for school records, and white to give to family. As a pompous twenty-three-year-old, completely sold on the new word-processing technology, I bragged about how I could write comments on the computer and press "PRINT" three times. I bragged about how I could organize all my grades on a spreadsheet and not calculate weighted averages by hand. The senior faculty mostly nodded and smiled. Only three of my gentle colleagues were doing the same, these three with greater wisdom than me, as they backed up their classroom data with hard copies regularly. I had greater faith in the computer than they did.

At the end of my second year teaching and bragging about my computer for which I had paid $400 in 1986, I opened my forty-megabyte hard drive labeled "C:" and entered all my grades. I was starting my first hard copy "backup" at the end of the semester. I pressed "PRINT" for the first time in four months, about three hours before grades were due.

The message came after about forty-five seconds: "FILE NOT FOUND."

I searched my computer files. There appeared to be no C: drive. It was as if my hard drive didn't exist. I tried every command I knew. I opened the box and looked in, not quite knowing what to look for, but thinking I'd look anyway. At least I felt as though I was doing something about the problem.

I quickly loaded up the large box computer into my old Volvo and drove down to the computer repair shop.

I was looking over the shoulder of the silent computer tech when I saw him type "FORMAT C:" on the keys.

"No!" I exclaimed with a guttural sound coming from deep in my chest.

The tech looked at me, blinked, and said, "Your data is long gone. I'm just checking to see if you have a functional hard drive." There was no emotion there, no understanding of the panic welling inside me.

I buried my head in my hands, breathing deeply. I needed a brown paper bag.

"Nope," he said flatly, "you have a very nice paperweight here." He removed the drive from the bowels of my white box computer, handed it to me with a thud, and reassembled the computer. He didn't even notice I was sweating and shaking. I had no records of any grades for the entire half year of school. To each of my sixty students, I gave a short quiz every day. I collected binders and gave a test every two weeks. The result: 60 students x 90 days + 60 students x 6 tests + 60 students x 6 binders = I didn't want to do the calculations. I had lost over 6,000 data points.

"And," he added, mechanically, "the warranty on the C: drive expired yesterday. Would you like to purchase a new one? It's $200 today."

This simply added insult to injury. A later check of paperwork would verify the unbelievable expiration date.

I did a little more math in my head as I sat dumbfounded next to the stone-faced tech. My monthly income was less than $700 per month. I still had a loan out on the computer, drive, and printer. I noted the value of a new forty-meg disc was now half of the year before. My faith in my significant investment—$1000 for the computer, $400 for the hard drive, plus extra for the dot-matrix printer—had plummeted. I did not have $200 for a new hard drive. I left the computer store, carrying my paperweight.

But I did have the strength to throw the old drive ten yards into an open dumpster down an alleyway.

I drove home slowly, not knowing what to do. I sat staring at my phone for a good fifteen minutes before I called the department chair and explained what had happened. I closed my eyes waiting for his response, knowing he typed his comments on a reliable Oliver No. 9 Bat Wing typewriter and recorded his grades in ink in his well-ruled gradebook.

After a short silence where I was sure he was questioning the wisdom of having hired me two years prior, he simply said, "You know your students well. I'm sure you can remember their grades well enough."

Did I? I knew the school policy was to have an eighty-five percent average grade in my classes. I knew students were acutely aware of their grades and calculated their own averages. This was a boarding school. Students had all left for home already, so I couldn't do something creative in class, such as ask them to record their expected grade on a three-by-five card.

So, after hanging up the phone, I sat by my class list and started writing numbers representing their grades, ranging from 60 to 98. I didn't feel as though I was guessing. If I was deciding between 82% and 83%, I chose the greater. Then I calculated the average: 85%. I felt as though I won the lottery. Double checking with a simple "reality check" like I ask my students to do on every problem, I thought my numbers fit the students' work.

I turned in the grades I had created and waited for the fallout.

But there was no fallout. Over the winter break, there were no phone calls. There were no letters to school administrators complaining about any of my submitted grades.

In January, my students shuffled in, taking their seats per usual and looking at me, expectantly.

"Welcome back, folks! It's so great to see you," I started. "I hope you had a wonderful, restful holiday." My holiday was not restful; I was worried sick about what complaints I might receive over the grades.

"I'd like to start this semester with a goal-setting task."

This task was my credibility check for my grades, but the students didn't need to know that. "On the three-by-five card in front of you, write your name at the top. Then record the numeric grade you expected to get last semester. If it's different from what you saw on your grade card, please address the difference on the card."

I breathed deeply. I was nervous. But I thought gathering more information could be helpful and would make them possibly less suspicious. "Below, write the grade you hope to earn this coming semester and what you intend to do to reach your goal."

As I collected the cards, I alphabetized them so I could easily compare the grades with the educated estimates I had made at the end of last semester. But as I read the student comments about their good intentions for the coming semester, I realized I had a gold mine of information.

Sue wrote, "I'll complete my homework every night," and Joe wrote, "I will ask my questions in class right when I have them instead of waiting," and Melvin wrote, "I'm going to come to the help sessions before tests this semester." I had insight into their individual needs and could hold each student accountable.

Later that night, I poured over the cards, comparing them to the grades I had assigned to them two weeks earlier. The numbers nearly matched. Those not matching were only one percentage point different. The students had no complaints, no surprises. The grades they received were the grades they expected and earned.

Teachers do know their students well—even new teachers who need to check their arrogance levels—*and* back up their files.

The Bright Red Inn

Spring 1987

"You'll have no problem finding a good hotel for you and your fifteen charges," they said. "It will be safe, easy, and inexpensive," they said. But they didn't know there would be a gem conference in Providence, Rhode Island that weekend. They didn't know nearly all hotels in a hundred-mile radius would be full. This was a decade before cell phones became mainstream, so the search for a hotel was more challenging then. But I was an overconfident new teacher.

We were visiting colleges in Providence. Some students were interested in Brown, others in Providence College. Some of my students were spending the night at these schools, generously hosted by students working with the admission offices. Most, however, were with me. Our plan was to check into a hotel for the night, review our college itinerary, and settle in with a movie. But "settling in" wasn't happening because I couldn't find a suitable hotel.

I'd stopped at about a dozen hotels; I was looking for five rooms: two for the six girls, two for the seven boys, and one for me. I needed to be sure the rooms, other than mine, had two large beds, so up to four kids could share one room. This was a tall order for this weekend of the big gem conference.

I pulled into the Bright Red Inn feeling hopeful and was relieved the hotel had rooms for us. It was only about an hour from town; it would do. I distributed the keys attached to large plastic fobs printed with the room numbers and reviewed the rules.

"Expectations for the night, folks," I started. "No boys visiting girls' rooms. No girls visiting boys' rooms. Best behavior—all school rules apply." Each teen nodded, gratefully accepted the key, and shuffled off to settle in. We all were tired.

I entered my room and found the bed appeared trapezoidal in shape and not rectangular. *At least there's not a mirror on the ceiling,* I thought…until I saw the mirror on the ceiling. I sat on the bed and heard a rasping squeak as it easily gave way beneath me. I was twenty-four—a soft bed would be fine, there was a deadbolt on the door, and I could close my eyes and not see the mirror. I washed off the layers on my skin from a day full of driving, playing mother hen, and scanning the horizon for "VACANCY" signs, then decided to check on the teens.

I called the rooms, one at a time. I heard Lily Tomlin in my head: *One-ringy-dingy, two-ringy-dingy,* and put the receiver down at *ten-ringy-dingy.* I shook my head, grabbed my coat, and headed out the door.

No one answered my knocks on the door of the first girls' room.

No one answered my bangs on the door of the second girls' room.

No one answered my bellows or bangs on the door of the first boys' room.

I inhaled and let my lungs fully inflate before I knocked on the last of the student rooms, but the door drifted open before I knocked. Students knew reversing the security bolt to prop the door open allowed anyone to walk in, and I did.

The entire group was sitting on the same double bed which sagged greatly. Each young person was fixated on the television, set to what sounded like an educational program by the tone of the woman's voice on the screen. No one noticed my entrance.

I looked at the screen and saw a scantily dressed buxom woman applying a condom to a broomstick.

My students groaned in unison when I stood in front of the screen with my hands on my hips.

After verifying with the front desk Channel 8 would no longer be available in any of the rooms I had rented, I completed a second check of my charges and called the administrator on duty at school in anticipation of fallout with parents.

"We'll talk about your hotel choice when you return to campus," said my friend, the administrator, after he thanked me for warning him about potential parent communications.

It's No Big Deal

1992

"It's no big deal," I said to my colleague, who was reaching out to me in case I needed comforting.

"Of course it wasn't; he's only fourteen," was his reply that we've laughed about for years.

Eddie was struggling in class but had decided to rally just prior to the spring final exam. About ten students had shown up for a review session the evening before the spring exam, including Eddie. Everyone else had left. I was gathering up my books from my desk, gently talking to Eddie. "It's good to see you making this effort, Eddie. I hope you will see success on the exam tomorrow."

Then I looked up to see him walking towards me, blocking the only exit. "Please," he said, looking between me and his exposed crotch.

In my college years, women were told to rehearse what they would do in an assault. "Make a plan," our teachers said. I remembered when one of my friends was assaulted, she repulsed and freaked out the attacker by dropping on all fours, barking, and lifting a leg to pee. Her plan was not only creative, but it was also successful.

My plan during college was vague: attack back, be loud, and use my fingernails and my knee. Like the slow motion that happens just prior to a car accident, my world slowed down as Eddie approached. I started to speak, "Put that—" when my mind went into teacher mode. This was a child who was hurting and making a poor choice. He needed therapy and help, not humiliation. He was swept up in the machismo culture of the era. So I spoke gently and with a pause in the middle, "Put that...away."

He didn't put it away. He continued to come at me.

"Please, Ms. Miller," he seemed to beg.

I dropped my books on the floor, pushed him aside—his hands were engaged, so this was easy—and strode swiftly out of the room.

I jumped in my car and drove to a friend's house. We went to dinner. As I considered the menu, I reviewed the events silently in my head. My memory felt surreal. *Did this really happen? It's too bizarre to be true.* I shared the evening's events with my friend. He said with the utmost certainty and urgency, "You need to report this."

Back in my apartment with my friend by my side, I was on the phone with the Dean of Students relaying the events. I was calm and methodical: "Eddie was at the review session tonight. At the end of the review session, I was telling him how happy I was he had chosen to work hard as the semester was coming to a close when he stood, unzipped his fly, pulled out his...erect penis, and—"

"*Stop,*" said the dean. "Could you repeat the last part? I'm not sure I heard you correctly." I had to repeat myself three times. This was not an ordinary expectation for my job as a teacher in a college-prep boarding school, even in the climate of the day. He finally allowed me to finish my story, including the, "Put that...away." In his wisdom, he immediately sent a private message to the school nurse, who was at my door before I hung up with him. I felt supported and heard.

The dean immediately went to Eddie, who admitted what he'd done without hesitation and completely corroborated my story. The dean phoned Eddie's parents, and they took the next flight to Colorado to pick him up.

"Are you pressing charges?" the nurse asked me.

I had not even considered the option. "Not if he gets help."

The nurse scheduled Eddie's emergency therapy visits for the next day.

It turned out, though, Eddie's parents had already left with him; he was AWOL. By the time the first therapy session was due to start, Eddie was over the Atlantic Ocean.

The next fall in my opening dorm meeting with my sixteen new charges, a young woman asked, "Ms. Miller, what should I do if I think I'm about to be raped?"

I started referring her to the school health educator, nurse, and counselor, when she said, "No, Ms. Miller, I don't want to see the nurse or counselor. We heard you were raped last year. What did you do? I want to know how to fight back."

"I wasn't raped," I said, curious about this rumor, and noting my palms were beginning to sweat.

"But Eddie...? The night before the exam...?"

School administrators told me not to discuss or address the events with Eddie to protect him. I was distressed that the reason I wasn't permitted to discuss what Eddie had done was to protect *him*. This simply wasn't fair to me or to the young women before me wanting to know how to fight back. I was frozen, so I repeated, "I was not raped."

I saw the young women in the room exchange glances, exhale, and show a "whatever" expression.

It was eleven p.m. I was up, either reading or writing comments in my living room. Fall Parent Weekend was always stressful because of the extra time required to spend with parents. I was expecting a long night, where I could take advantage of the quiet and dark campus to get a little ahead in my class preparation. In my third year teaching, I was spending many hours preparing for class.

Then, there was a rather insistent knock on my apartment door. Usually, students who need me would knock on the door leading directly into the dorm. The knocking was on my outside door, next to a driveway passing close to my front door. While a knock at eleven at night wasn't a surprise or unbelievable, what happened next left me somewhere between shaking my head and wondering if it really happened.

Mr. Nova, the parent of a student earning a C in my math class, was at my door. Mr. Nova was physically imposing. He worked out and had a full head of lush yellow hair and film-star features. He wore a button-down linen shirt with the top three or four buttons left open. He was a single parent.

I cracked the door. "Yes?"

"Ms. Miller, I'm concerned about how my son is doing in your class."

"Um, Mr. Nova, it's eleven p.m. We can discuss your son during the day."

"I wanted to talk with you *now* so I could offer you something."

Offer me something? I began to squirm a little.

"Mr. Nova, this is not appropriate. We can talk in the morning about your son's progress in math class."

He looked at me deeply. His hands were in front of his chest, cupped with palms together in the position of "hamburger" in sign language. "I will do anything—*anything*—to have him be successful in math class. Let me repeat, *anything*." His eyebrows were slightly drawn, and he looked at me imploringly.

"Good night, Mr. Nova." I closed the door, clicked the lock, turned out my living room light, and retired to the recesses of my apartment.

Perhaps I misunderstood? But it was eleven o'clock. The campus was quiet and dark. The next day, I decided to share news of my late-night visitor with some colleagues who were also friends.

"Mr. Nova, Taylor's dad, arrived at my apartment at eleven o'clock last night..."

My colleagues, Marge and Henry, looked at each other, confused. "Perhaps he was looking for the theater. It's right next to your front door?"

"No, it was eleven p.m. There was no theater performance. And he clearly was wanting *me*. What should I do now?"

Henry stood up, "Time for class."

Marge scoffed and said, "Hard to believe."

"Yes, it is," I said as I looked down. *Did this really happen?* I was doubting myself.

The next day at a private table during lunch, Henry began the conversation. "You know, several of us were talking, and we simply don't believe this happened."

Shocked they thought I might have created this story, I said, "Whether or not you believe it happened doesn't change the fact that it happened." Now it was my turn to leave abruptly.

In the years following, I've mulled over my colleagues' disbelief in Mr. Nova's late-night appearance at my door. I never followed up with school administrators or asked for support to guarantee my safety.

A crack formed in my relationship with Marge and Henry that became deeper with time. I'm sure students have similar stories about the distress endured when their stories are not believed. Progress towards healing requires being listened to and trusted.

Words Matter

1985: I wanted the job. I was a senior in college, an econ major, and interviewing with big-name companies for positions in finance, management, and economic analysis. I sat in the chair opposite the interviewer, ankles crossed, knees together, spine erect.

"We have never had a girl in this job. What makes you think you are up to it?"

Pretty sure this was not a legal question for him to ask, I was not sure how to proceed. I wanted to walk out.

"You'd be well served to have *women* in your ranks. You'll note my academic record rivals, parallels, or exceeds your other applicants for this post." *Nailed it,* I thought.

"I see you're a psychology major. We don't hire psychology majors." He clearly was cherry-picking my resume, trying hard to discredit me.

"You'll note I have two majors—one in economics and one in psychology. Therefore, I exceed your requirements and have more skills and understanding to offer because of my added area of academic study. I'm sure you're aware of the organizational skills required in double-majoring as well." *Nailed it again,* I thought.

I left the interview with a firm handshake and great uncertainty. *Why am I trying to dig myself out of a hole with each question? Why do I feel as though I didn't actually nail it?*

After the interview, my 500-level seminar entitled The Economics of Discrimination was starting too soon for me to return to my dorm to shed my interview clothing, so I arrived still dressed in a pencil skirt, matching jacket, blouse, stockings, and pumps. I slid into the chair-desk combo and looked around at my peers in jeans and t-shirts. Their loud, low voices made it more difficult for me to be heard, but when only male pronouns were being used to describe managers and their decisions, I had a sudden revelation and knew I had to speak loudly about it.

"When you all are discussing a manager, what physical characteristics appear in the image in your mind?" I waited, then listened intently to each of their responses.

"I see a tall man in a pin-striped suit with thinning hair."

"He's blonde, clean-shaven, broad chested, built like a boxer."

"Hey, this is a seminar on discrimination—I'm seeing a black man in a white shirt, dark jacket, and tie."

"Yeah, I can imagine a Hispanic guy with a mustache."

They nodded at each other, the last two smiling and thinking, *Nailed it*. After all, they were in a class about discrimination.

Then it was my turn. "Anyone see a woman?"

Silence.

It was so quiet I could hear their thoughts: *Oops*.

"So, let's begin using gender-neutral pronouns or consciously using feminine pronouns. I think it makes a difference. I just came from an interview with Millicent Steel Investments. If my interviewer never imagined a woman in the job for which I was applying, then I don't have a shot in hell of getting the job." Never before had I been so outspoken about inclusive language. My classmates agreed to be conscious of their language and what images they held in their heads of people in management.

1992: Later in my career as a teacher, I continued my quest for inclusive language. The nineties were still early in the quest for gender-inclusive language; I couldn't help but think perhaps the reason the administrator didn't see me in the role of department chairman was because of the gender specificity of the title. When I earned the position of chair, only a little nudging—and a year's time—was necessary to adjust the language in the faculty handbook. It took a little longer for the spoken language to follow suit.

My next school placement had a more diverse Academic Committee, comprised of department "chairmen," roughly half of them women. But the language did not follow suit. The assistant "headmaster" balked at changing the language because of the effort required.

"I'm happy to word process the document to make smooth and inclusive language for all roles at the school," I tried.

Mr. Neff lowered his head so I could see his full pate and laughed softly. "You know, Jean, it's so important to pick the right battles at a school. You won't be able to win all your battles. This one just isn't important, and I'd hate to see you cashing in all your chips for something as trivial as language in the handbook."

Later in the same year, the "headmaster" and his wife were hosting a set of visiting Heads of School from independent schools around the city. Several women heads were in attendance. His wife stood to make a toast, "To all the headmasters!" She glowed.

Someone nudged her and hissed, "Heads of School, *not* headmasters." She replied so all could hear, "No, I do mean the headmasters! Let them rise so we can honor them." The women Heads of School looked around the room at each other and shifted uncomfortably.

GAFFO to GAFCATS

Spring 1987

"What's GAFFO?" I asked innocently. My colleagues looked anywhere but at me, picked at their nails, and shifted in their chairs. We were at lunch in the dining hall. Some spooned heaps of food into their mouths so they couldn't speak.

"I need to go to class," said one.

"Just a student club," said another.

"Is there a sponsor? What's the mission?" I asked. I was one of the newest faculty members and was still learning about the school programs. I looked from person to person, but not one of the men would catch my eye.

Then the topic changed quickly to politics. George Bush and Michael Dukakis were running for president in the 1988 election year. Teachers at residential schools are so busy coaching, doing dorm duty, preparing for class, counseling kids, and teaching, we never read as much as we'd like and often rely on each other to share what snippets we've heard on NPR. I was okay with changing the topic away from school events; lunch was a small escape from the rigors of our career.

"Neither candidate seems strong or decisive," I said, referencing something I had heard about the Republicans trying, unsuccessfully, to find a candidate as charismatic as Reagan.

"I dunno," replied a young English teacher, "I've been a *bush* fan for about twelve years now." He openly chuckled, unable to deadpan the joke.

Most of the time, I was unaware I was the only female at the lunch table. But today, as my eyes rested on the chuckling faces of my male colleagues around the table, I was very aware of my skirt, my blouse, the hair strand slipping out from behind my ear—my gender. I picked up my tray and walked towards the bussing area, hearing their "heh-heh-heh" sounds fade as I moved further away. My hips burned. *Were they watching me walk? If I felt this way, how did the young and impressionable girls feel?*

Years later, I would learn appropriate vocabulary to describe what I was experiencing: "Hostile Work Environment." In 1987, I tried to develop my own vocabulary to reflect my discomfort.

"I'm really bothered by the locker room talk happening in the dining hall during the school day," I relayed to the Assistant Head of School before describing the "bush" comment.

"Jean, I appreciate what you are saying, but you simply can't handle a clever double entendre," he replied. "You might think about developing a thicker skin. You don't need to be so sensitive about these clever jokes."

"What about the catcalls around campus?" I asked. The male students had taken to whistling at the female students across campus grounds.

"It's not really a problem," he replied. "It's how they get the girls' attention. I think the girls like it."

"I think many don't like it. If they do, then they have learned the wrong lesson."

He shrugged at my reply.

Despite being admonished to develop a "thicker skin," I developed a thinner skin. I became highly sensitive to events around campus and noticed how boys traveling in the school vans concocted sing-song poetry about attractive faculty and sexual positions as the male faculty driver laughed. I noticed the domination of boys' participation in class, athletic awards solely for boys in the All-School Meetings, and how the girls watched the boys' events but not vice versa.

"Encourage your guy friends to watch you play field hockey," I'd say to the girls in the dorm.

"They aren't interested," came the reply. "Girls' sports just aren't as interesting." In my mailbox, I received an anonymous clipping from a newspaper editorial—no specific source visible—explaining how no one wanted to watch women's tennis because it was boring. Clearly, the sender had not seen Billy Jean King, Steffi Graf, Margaret Court, or Martina Navratilova play. Also, this was before the Williams sisters became household names.

Hearing no response from my male colleagues about the meaning of GAFFO, I decided to ask the girls in the dorm one evening. They became angry. Explosive. They interrupted each other, citing demeaning comments, sexual references, unwanted attention, "snow baths," and snowball attacks. It dawned on me that the boys did not know how to give appropriate attention to the new female members of their community.

"But what does GAFFO stand for?" I naively asked. Susan looked at Florence. Florence looked at Chrissy. Chrissy looked at Jess.

"I'm not telling her," said Florence with a shake of her head. Susan and Jess looked embarrassed.

Of course, Chrissy's superpower was her frank and honest speech. "You really want to know? It means *Girls Are for F***ing Only.*"

With ice in my veins and meat on the bone, I marched to the Head of School's office. He needed to know what was happening on campus. The school had been coed for about ten years. We all could expect challenges, but these challenges needed addressing immediately and with strength. I saw my purpose at the school with more conviction than I had ever previously mustered about any topic.

In the administrative building, I marched past the assistant's office as she called after me, "What is your business, Jean?" I saw Mr. Block's office door open and let myself in. He rose to greet me.

With a single hand movement, I swung the heavy hand-adzed door closed and looked at him firmly.

"Hello, Jean," he said tentatively, gesturing towards a chair next to the fireplace. On the mantle was a clay owl decorated by an Acoma artist. I could not sit.

Without formality or introduction, I began speaking in single words with a full two seconds between each word. "*Do…you…know…what…GAFFO…stands…for?*"

"It's one of the boys' groups on campus, isn't it? Like a social club?"

"*Girls Are for F***ing Only,*" I tried not to yell. Not being successful, I took a deep breath and spoke again in a more measured tone, "Girls are for f***ing only."

"Oh no," he said. The color drained from his face. "Oh no," he repeated.

I collapsed into the chair by the fireplace. He sat next to the painted owl. We sat together, listening to my heavy breathing.

He waited for me to calm myself, then began slowly. "I need to think about what to do. We need to make a plan. Do you think the other women on campus would be interested in joining a conversation?"

Following our discussion, Mr. Block convened the seven women on the faculty in his home one cold evening in the spring of 1987. He scribbled notes voraciously as we recounted concerns, told stories, and brainstormed solutions. After eleven p.m., we emerged bleary-eyed but energized. At the bottom of the stairs leading out of his apartment, we were deflated after seeing someone had posted a large sign on a pole: "GAFFO RULES." The female college counselor said, "Those boys must feel threatened right now." We quietly pulled down similar signs outside of our own apartments when we returned home.

Later in the spring, I was in the middle of class when I was jarred into a different consciousness. I saw a large poster advertising beer, featuring a buxom, well exposed "St. Pauli Girl" displayed on the south wall of my classroom. A colleague with whom I shared the classroom had hung the poster on the wall as an example of propaganda. In a moment of clarity, I saw it for what it was—a beer ad demeaning to women. *I'll remove it after class,* I thought to myself. Ironically, I was teaching Freudian Theory in my psychology class. But just as class ended, three young women approached me.

"Are you really okay with that poster on the wall? I don't like it," Jennifer began.

"Yeah, it's about beer," said one accomplice.

Jennifer was impatient with her peer. "It objectifies women! And as our only outspoken feminist teacher on campus, I can't believe you allow it to be on your wall." She scoffed. Jennifer was one of the smartest people I knew and had a steely character. She had a commanding presence even at her young age—and still does now as a professor at a prominent university.

The third young woman, Liz, known for her sharp intellect, sparse use of speech, calm affect, and direct approach, eyed me with certainty. "I can chat with Dr. Allen, the chair of the department, and the administration."

I knew I had to choose my words carefully to maintain everyone's dignity. "I'm sure Dr. Allen has a reason for displaying this poster. Let's take it down now, and I'll discuss it with him later." He was not in his office, so I left the rolled up, offensive poster on his desk and made my way to my next class.

Dr. Allen was a dear colleague, a brilliant man, and a valued educator. He taught U.S. and European history classes like intellectual history courses, rather than high-school style courses that recited lists of events. He led energizing discussions and supported students in their efforts to think and write better. He mentored me with grace and kindness, even serving on the committee approving my graduate thesis. He wrote beautifully, like the Ivy League graduate he was. However, he was a product of his time, location, and experience. He didn't see anything wrong with language, images, and jokes starting to be recognized as deeply troublesome. I believed I could have a civil conversation about our concerns once we both had a few minutes together. I figured I'd catch up with him after my Geometry class.

After forty-five minutes of proving triangles congruent, I began to walk towards Dr. Allen's office. Then I heard my name bellowed from the direction of the administration building down the hill. I stopped and walked in his direction.

Dr. Allen was famous for a colorful vocabulary—I remember opening a thesaurus to a random page and joking with a colleague, "Look, there's Dr. Allen's vocabulary."

I didn't hear all his words when he came within earshot, but I remember "high-handed," "inappropriate," "preemptory," "haughty," and "pompous" as he gestured wildly with his arms going up to the sky and then down at my feet. His face was red, and spittle sprayed periodically from his mouth. He was angry I had taken down his poster. He ended his tirade with sending me to the Dean of Faculty's office "immediately." I was frozen in place but aware of others walking past us on their way to class. He had chosen to make a public display of his anger.

I was glad to leave him and felt self-righteous as I walked into the dean's office, sure I'd be vindicated because the poster was clearly repulsive.

The dean had a verbal scythe he used to remove my legs below the knees, my arms, my tongue, and my memory of his specific words. In short, he agreed with Dr. Allen. Dr. Allen was, of course, a senior faculty member.

I returned to my apartment, pulled out my oversized Naugahyde brown suitcase, and began packing. I would head to my parent's house across the country in my little orange Volvo loaded with a few basics. I was fine with leaving my linens, kitchen items, a couple random posters, and difficult memories of my first six months as a teacher. I was thankful for supportive and loving parents who would welcome me and bring me peace. If the adults here thought posters displaying the St. Pauli Girl's breasts, whistling at attractive young women, and jokes about bush were all appropriate, then it was clear this was not a place I belonged. The energy I felt after the meeting in Mr. Block's apartment had dissipated.

Meanwhile, Dr. Allen continued his St Pauli Girl poster rant in the history department office as our colleagues sat in horror. When Dr. Allen left the office, one young faculty member picked up the poster roll, opened it to see the grinning cheeks on the curly-haired blonde, and swore under his breath. After taking the poster to the administration building and sharing it with the dean, the young faculty member arrived at my apartment door.

He found me packing. "The dean agrees with you—it's not an appropriate poster for a classroom."

"I can't stay here," I said between sobs.

"You must," he said. "We desperately need you. Our students need you."

That caused me pause.

I stayed for six years, then returned about ten years later for another four.

In 2022, the Board of Trustees offered a contract to a highly qualified woman to serve as the new Head of School. So now, GAFFO has become GAFCATS: *Girls Are for Calling All the Shots.*

Swim Team

1986

The first swim team I coached was full of energetic and fun ninth-grade girls. A highlight of my day was heading down to the pool for practice and spending time with them in the afternoon.

We started workouts with the warmup I endured in high school: 500 swim, 500 kick, 500 pull. They whined at the kicks. "Do we have to, Coach M.?" asked Fern. I was Ms. M. in class, "Jean" behind my back, and "Coach M." on the pool deck. I had remembered making the same complaint to my coach but wasn't going to let them know.

I began to record the full workout on the chalkboard, but noticed Fern was using the 500 kick as an opportunity to have a gossip session with Emily and Natalie. They were three abreast in the same lane, kicking slowly with their heads resting on the kickboards, and talking in hushed tones. Natalie was, of course, animated; Fern was running the show from the middle position; Emily was giggling and listening. *Board meetings,* I thought.

"You know," I said loudly, "kicking helps give definition to your abdominals, but only if you work it." They split up their triad. I said this whenever I saw them slacking, and they always stopped whining and increased their efforts.

Each year, we ordered new team racing suits. In my gross inexperience, I pulled out the catalogue in the commons room of the dorm during a duty night. We were all looking and pointing at pictures of slender and striking non-swimmer models in the glossy pages. I stepped back to listen to them discuss what they wanted in a bathing suit.

"Oh, look at that one! The stripes make your boobs look bigger," said one girl.

"Oh, I like this one—the red and black horizontal stripes are rad," said the tallest girl on the team.

"What about that one? The dark color at the bottom will make my butt look smaller," said the girl with the generous derriere.

Then they became louder. Some of the girls became irrationally committed to one suit or another, mostly based upon how it complemented their favorite or least favorite body part. I could hear voices becoming sharp and louder. *Uh-oh*, I thought. *What to do?*

I leaned over the opened page, pointed to one suit randomly and said, "That one will make us all look slender." Soon they all pointed to my choice with enthusiasm and discussions ended.

Upon recounting this story the following day to my peers, we had a good laugh. It took time—and my own maturation—to become embarrassed that I had contributed to the perpetuation of the 1980s' culture that promoted unrealistically slender and damaging physical ideals in young women.

The 500 yard freestyle event was the longest race in our high school swimming program. Natalie's swimming style and athleticism fit the 500 to a "T," but she didn't seem to be so sure. In the days before the meet, I bolstered her, letting her know I had faith in her training and skills. She would do well. About five minutes before the 500 on race day, I handed Natalie a card with her name, event, and heat identified. She was to present the card to the official just before her race. "You'll do great. Go get 'em." Then I looked down to be sure my watch was set, adjust my papers, and ready myself to record her splits.

"Um, Coach M.?" I heard a small voice report to my right. "We can't find Natalie, and she's supposed to be swimming." Emily looked worried. I looked around frantically. Natalie was not on the deck.

"Hold the race," I asked the ref, who pursed his lips and nodded no. Putting down my clipboard, I ran into the bathroom—no Natalie. I searched around the lockers—no Natalie. The shower room appeared empty, but I pulled a curtain to the side and found her hiding, standing upright in a swim cap with goggles on her forehead, fingernails in her mouth, and body fully tensed. I reached out to her, and she grabbed me, unable to speak. She was shaking.

"Go slow," I said. "Just finish. That's all. And you know what? You've never done this race before, so it will be your personal best!"

With pressure released but still a struggling mindset, she approached the blocks and dove in at the start. The only goal I had set for her was to finish. I stayed with her, signaling her from the sidelines and encouraging Fern and Emily to swing a white towel so Natalie could see it during the race. She stayed steady with two other swimmers, each vying for first place. As swimmers approached length sixteen, with a hundred yards to go, the other competitors began to slip back, but Natalie's training and determination kicked in. Her stroke remained strong and she moved ahead, snapping each flip turn with an "I dare you" to her competitors. She finished at least three yards ahead of second place. Her teammates responded with whoops, hollers, and hugs. Natalie was beaming. I pulled her into a hug, "You did it!"

Determination was in her eyes. "I wasn't going to let them get ahead of me. I'm better than they are."

Two days later in All-School Meeting, I stood to announce the results of the meet. Of course, I identified all first-place winners, including Natalie. Immediately following, she ran to me and said, "Don't ever do that again."

"Do what?" I asked.

"I don't want you to say my name in All-School Meeting *ever* again. I don't care that the boys get their names read—the girls don't need names read." She was a little frantic. *Oh*, I thought. *This is a gender issue*. I filed a couple ideas away in the back cabinet of my brain. Clearly this needed addressing.

Girls in boarding schools often throw modesty to the wind. I walked through the communal showers after practice each day and found myself moving quickly through their space. One day, I couldn't help but notice—each had a brand-new tattoo on her hip. Natalie had a Grateful Dead bear she proudly displayed as she jumped to the beat of a Grateful Dead tune. Fern had a moon and star—"But look, it smeared, so I got it for free." Emily had a dove, and Lissa had an olive branch—"We couldn't both afford a full 'dove with olive branch' tattoo, so we split it. We figure we'll each finish them down the road and have identical tattoos later."

How some establishment in downtown Colorado Springs put tattoos on underaged girls escapes me, but there they were.

"You all know you'll have these for the rest of your lives, don't you?" I stupidly asked, not knowing what else to say.

"Yes, isn't that super cool? We will always have this connection to each other," Lissa said as they all nodded in agreement. I was convinced this would be discovered and somehow, as their dorm parent, teacher, and swim coach, I'd be fired.

Before the last meet of the season, I looked at the four swimmers' 100 yard freestyle times, then looked again. I compared their times to the 400 free relay record up on the record board. I double and triple checked. *They could do this*, I thought. It was the last meet of the season. The 400 yard freestyle relay was the final event. What a great ending this could be!

"You know, you could break the school record," I quietly said.

"I'm tired," said Fern.

"Someone else will break it down the road," said Natalie.

"Meh," said Emily.

Cathy just shrugged. Cathy was a serious swimmer, the fastest, and our MVP for two years. She knew she couldn't do this on her own, but she'd be swimming anchor and would certainly do her best.

"Don't you want to break the record? Having your names on the record board would be so cool!" I was working too hard to drum up enthusiasm. Cathy nodded with interest and agreement, as if to say, "Keep going, Coach M."

The team seemed to be just going through the motions of finishing the season during the last meet. The gears were spinning in my head during the meet, trying to put myself in their shoes and find a way to light a fire in them, to help them have their names on the record board for the 400 relay.

I stood with them behind the blocks in the two minutes before the 400 relay. They were talking boys or weekend plans or who failed room inspections or what they wanted to order from the local cafe.

"I'll shave my legs if you break the record," I said quietly.

All four stopped moving, stopped chatting, and looked at me, frozen in time and space.

"What?" asked Fern. "For real?"

"And your armpits," said quick-thinking Natalie.

I nodded affirmative, raising an eyebrow.

Cathy showed a hopeful expression. Maybe they would be able to do this.

Suddenly, all four young women were energized. Their oversized eyes lit up our small circle behind the starting blocks. "Let's do this," Emily said. Cathy flapped her arms, slapping her triceps against her lats as fast swimmers are known to do. Fern and Natalie began jumping up and down, wiggling their arms to warm up.

The gun went off. They sprinted like they never had before. When Cathy came to the wall ending the event, they had completely shattered the record. There was an eruption of uncontrolled screaming and carrying-on by swimmers and teammates.

Fern arched herself backwards with loud, unintelligible sounds coming from her mouth. Emily jumped up and down. Cathy grinned. Natalie pointed at me, "You have to shave!"

"Just don't jump or fall in the water before the last swimmer comes to the wall or you'll be disqualified," I warned them, watching their feet moving quickly on the slippery pool deck.

With hand gestures, they seemed to push my words aside and Natalie echoed, "You have to *shave!*" They were not excited about breaking the record—they were thrilled I was going to have to fulfill my promise of shaving.

Now it was my turn. I had long ignored Natalie's demand I stop offering awards or discussing their athletic prowess during the All-School Meetings. The swimmers learned that I was relentless in publicly promoting their successes and thus developed a tolerance to my singing their praises with enthusiastic announcements.

I walked slowly to the podium and adjusted the microphone. "We had a big meet on Saturday—Natalie, Fern, Emily, and Cathy broke the school record in the 400 free relay." People cheered wildly. Each young woman came forward to accept an envelope and gold ribbon I had prepared to mark her success. Each was beaming, proud of her accomplishment, and gazed out at her peers cheering for her. Indeed, the whole school was cheering for them.

When my announcement was over, we each returned to our seats and sat quietly. I was waiting, working hard to suppress a grin. My hands sat loosely on my lap, holding the notes I used as reference during the award announcement.

Behind me, I heard it begin during an announcement about the school schedule. A loud, "No!" from Natalie. Then each young woman gave a guttural sound that would be an expletive if she knew she could get away with it. And my body shook with uncontrollable laughter.

The envelopes each contained a card proclaiming success. Taped to the card was a collection of small, fine hairs.

The Debate

Spring 1987

My take-home salary gave me less than $700 each month. Two hundred tickets at $2.50 spends $500 of those dollars before the month begins.

At a local college, famous conservative politician Phyllis Schlafly was debating Sarah Weddington of Roe v. Wade fame. Tickets were inexpensive, even for 1987, at $2.50 and would sell fast in a college environment. I wanted to bring as many students as wanted to attend, and I needed to be first in line to purchase the tickets. Waiting a week to determine interest in the event would mean there would be no tickets left to purchase. There were about 220 enrolled students at the school.

I must have faith, I kept thinking.
I must have faith students will want to go.
I must have faith my colleagues will support this idea.
I must have faith I'll be able to get my money back.

The Greek philosopher Heraclitus is famous for saying, "There is nothing permanent except change." I was just hoping the change went in the right direction.

I certainly could not afford to spend $500, however, I could not afford to miss the opportunity of exposing my beloved students to Mrs. Schlafly debating Ms. Weddington.

So, I purchased two hundred tickets, maxing out my Visa limit of $500.

Nervous, I stood in front of the school during our weekly All-School Meeting.

"Anyone know who Sarah Weddington is?"

Silence.

Some people nodded their heads in either fatigue or a desire to please the speaker. Some were looking down, picking at their nails. Members of the faculty stared straight ahead.

"Sarah Weddington is the lawyer who successfully argued Roe v. Wade to the Supreme Court in the early 1970s within two years of finishing law school. Her success is the reason women enjoy freedom of choice in their doctors' offices."

The girls looked right at me.

"Anyone know who Phyllis Schlafly is?"

Silence.

"Mrs. Schlafly is every conservative's answer to the Equal Rights Amendment. She's an anti-feminist spokesperson for the political right. She believes feminism has made women unhappy. She is an accomplished woman—a wife, mother, activist, lawyer, columnist, author, radio host—but her biggest claim to fame is successfully leading a campaign of conservative women with the goal of blocking the ERA. She thinks women would be happier stabilizing the household, raising children, putting dinner on the table, and supporting their husbands."

I could hear people shifting in their seats, and I could see scrunched up, disbelieving faces looking at each other, saying, "What?"

I continued, "Sarah Weddington and Phyllis Schlafly are debating each other at the college in town." I looked around the room. All eyes were on me and listening. "I have secured two hundred tickets at $2.50 each. If you'd like to go, sign up with me after the meeting. First come, first served."

My collection of tickets sold out in less than ten minutes, with some reserved for faculty members who would drive the school buses. An excess of faculty volunteered to drive.

By the afternoon of the highly anticipated debate, the history teachers and dorm parents had shared further information about these two powerful women with students. Everyone was prepared to hear a lively and testy debate.

Students arrived early to load onto the busses, making sure they could sit with their friends. I was with the young women from my dorm. Their chitchat on the bus was animated.

"It's only been thirteen years since the abortion decision—can you believe it?"

"Does she really believe women should stay home with the kids—I mean—she doesn't."

"I can't wait to hear two women lawyers go at it."

"Do you think they will swear at each other?"

"Do you think there will there be protesters there?"

I stayed quiet. These fifteen-year-olds were entering a college environment, in a room filled with volatile and liberal college students discussing a mature topic. I didn't know how my charges would respond. Thankful for my supportive colleagues driving busses and sitting with our students, I tried to relax and listen to the high-pitched voices behind me in the bus.

We shuffled into a large, banquet-style room with plastic chairs arranged in rows. The well-lit stage had two podiums embossed with the college logo. Our arrival time and the open-seating tickets meant we had seats in the back third of the room, mostly together. I chose to stay with the youngest in our group. I was playing mother hen with the girls in our dorm whom I had come to care deeply about.

The style of the debate was not formal. There were no pre-planned questions thrown at the lawyers with timed responses. Each woman had the opportunity to speak. It dawned on me this paired talk was a circuit they were doing together at college campuses, with written and well-planned speeches to address topics about which they vehemently disagreed. Mrs. Schlafly opened, discussing the role of the successful woman. Each characteristic was framed in terms of a husband and how important women were in the effort to raise healthy children and to keep the men in the family happy.

Glancing to my left and right, I saw my students leaning forward, jaws slack, hands on knees. Some of their faces were beginning to turn red. These ideas were novel to them.

Ms. Weddington countered, discussing women as intelligent, valuable contributors to society who could make their own decisions. Women needed to be regarded respectfully and paid at the same level as men. She pointed out that a woman earned an average of sixty-seven cents to each dollar a man earned.

Now Mrs. Schlafly's turn—she took a minute to purse her lips, tilt her bouffant-topped head to her right, and chuckle. "Oh, Mrs. Weddington, I bet your husband is so unhappy." She shook her head slowly, wearing a sad smile. She looked down and to the right. Judging by the age gap and the tone, Mrs. Schlafly could be Ms. Weddington's mother.

Some of the women in the audience stood and started to speak out, defending Ms. Weddington. "That's ridiculous!"

"But ladies," Mrs. Schlafly said, addressing the audience in her saccharine voice, "you don't want to make your husbands unhappy by earning more money than them, do you? They want to provide for you. Admit it's *most* important to keep your husbands happy."

At this, my student Natalie joined the college women in the room standing on their chairs. Her face was red. She was pointing and screaming somewhat unintelligibly at Mrs. Schlafly. Her bold actions encouraged her peers to stand on chairs, too. Soon, Natalie was joined by Fern and Rose and Lissa—yelling, sweating, and screaming.

Sure we were going to get kicked out by the security guards, I moved behind their chairs, encouraging them to sit, calm down, and listen. They were not having it. I looked around frantically—nearly every young woman was standing on her chair yelling. One of my charges, Emily, appeared a little bewildered, overwhelmed, and still surprised. She chose to sit still amid the near complete lack of decorum demonstrated by her peers. I shrugged slightly and stood quietly next to Emily, feeling very proud of the young people who I accompanied on this field trip.

The "debate" continued, alternating between Mrs. Schlafly and Ms. Weddington. Members of the audience participated as one, standing up and alternating between yelling at Mrs. Schlafly, who specialized in her condescending smile, and yelling, "Yeah!" at anything Ms. Weddington said.

When Ms. Weddington spoke for the last time, she urged the audience to get involved and to stay involved. These all were important issues, and it was important all voices were heard. "Remember your feelings tonight," she said. "You can't rely on me or Gloria Steinem to stand up for you your whole life. We need a strong advocate from your ranks."

Invigorated, enraged, animated, and still flushed, we filtered out of the room. I checked people into the busses, and we traveled back to the dorms. I listened to their loud voices.

"She has a job! She's a hypocrite!"

"Is this the real world? Do others think this way?"

"There's so much I didn't know about how people think."

"I want to be a doctor. Is she telling me I shouldn't be a doctor because it would take away time from my family? What if I don't want a family?"

Part 3:
Trails and Trials

"Earth and sky, woods and fields, lakes and rivers, the mountain, and the sea, are excellent school masters, and teach us more than we can ever learn from books."

– *John Lubbock*

Shinrin Yoku is a Japanese term translated loosely as "forest bathing" and is the practice of bringing nature into daily experience as part of a quest for health, happiness, and peace. Taking students on outdoor experiences allows them to understand the benefits of *Shinrin Yoku*, but also permits novel learning experiences transcending the standard classroom experience. Multi-day hiking or camping experiences require group connection, cooperation, communication, and problem solving. An outdoor educational experience is a powerful means for developing connections, group work skills, and learning self-reliance.

As a teacher, some of my most memorable experiences are from outdoor and experiential adventures. When I started teaching, little did I know how important these adventures would be.

Whether swimming with students in Alcatraz, camping in the Sangre de Cristo mountains, or having a "Great Sit" in the classroom, living and learning together in close proximity creates a daily intensity that accelerates the progression of maturation, relationships, and growth. Simple and seemingly mundane tasks start to take on great importance and create a deep mutual experience.

While daily mundane tasks are deeply meaningful, the more profound events that inevitably arise—loss, injury, great successes and failures—ultimately become life-defining and unforgettable. My years spent in a boarding school included all aspects of the human story, be they mundane or powerful, wondrous or terrible, perspicuous or subtle. Compounded by the electricity and chemistry of developing minds, bodies, and spirits, skilled teachers instinctively approach each event with cautious care, deliberate delicacy, layers of love, and heaps of humor.

The times we are most fragile and vulnerable are times we are most able to grow and become stronger and capable of greater clarity. Paired with healthy habits and relationships built upon experiences, such as trips in the forest together, we are reminded to lean on each other, problem solve, and breathe in the beauty around us.

Backpacking with Jim

Fall 1987

A camping novice at the beginning of my second year teaching in a boarding school, I was a little concerned when the administration placed me on a three-day orientation adventure for twenty students. The co-leader of the trip was Jim, the boys' swim coach and a well-seasoned educator who had spent time in the wilderness with a pack on his back. I was young and athletic. I had a co-leader who knew what he was doing. Certainly, between the two of us, we'd be okay.

The day was sunny. The students grew tired after the first twenty minutes. Jim took more and more weight onto his pack and looked like a face on a Winnebago. I was carrying all I could and was thankful for his strength and patience.

A student approached me quietly with a private concern. "Juan says he doesn't have his sleeping bag. What are we going to do?" I had remembered checking the kids' gear; surely I would have noticed the missing bag. I made my way up the trail to Juan.

"Juan, do you have your sleeping bag?" Juan was a polite young man, an exchange student from Ecuador, who flashed me a smile and said he did not have his sleeping bag. Then he ran on ahead. Jim was at the end of the line of hikers. I let others pass until I could privately present the problem.

"Juan does not have his sleeping bag; let's make a plan." We brainstormed about extra clothing, "making" a bag from our down coats, and other options. It was too late to head back. Sleeping at 11,000 feet would be chilly at any time of year. Our plan was for me to sleep in a "bag" constructed of our excess clothing. I was worried about being cold and my mind organized how I would layer my clothing for the night and seal up the gap between Jim's down jacket and mine.

As someone from New England who thought of a mountain as something rising one thousand feet above the valley floor, I marveled, and still marvel, at the crags and real mountains of the Rockies rising to fourteen thousand feet, often eight thousand feet above the valley floor.

Our train of hikers arrived at the first camping spot after a vertical ascent of over 2,500 feet. Above tree line, small patches of snow left over from the last winter contrasted with the blue of a calm alpine lake. Comanche Peak loomed overhead backed by a clear blue sky. We all were very hot, and the water looked refreshing. The students began stripping down to their skivvies and whooping as they headed toward the lake.

Jim's booming voice seemed to be coming from an intercom when he demanded they stop. They froze in place, then returned to form a semicircle in front of him. He reviewed the rules we had established at the start of the adventure, including asking permission before venturing off. They sat quietly. Then he said, "You may go swim, but keep in mind the water's really cold, and it will rain this afternoon. Please set up your tents and prepare for rain *before* you swim."

Eyes rolled. Some of the boys snorted. "But Mr. Jim, the sky's blue! It won't rain!" They didn't heed his advice and sprinted out towards the lake instead.

Jim and I set up our tents, rolled out our sleeping pads, gathered firewood to put under a tarp, and looked out at our young hikers, now shivering with a chill from the lake and not noticing the gathering dark clouds. A gust of wind brought the first few drops; Jim and I went into one of our tents to wade out the storm together. I looked at my watch: 3:00. We still had a couple hours before dinner would need to be prepared. Chuckling, we listened to the rain on our tent fly and to the kids running around outside in the mud in their skivvies trying to set up their tents. Their voices increased in volume so they could hear each other over the drumming rain. Setting up the tents didn't go so well. I was glad to have listened to Jim and to have an experienced colleague.

Soon we heard a wee voice, "Knock, knock?" Jim and I looked at each other. "Yeeeessss?" asked Jim slowly.

"We are freezing and wet. Can we come in?"

Jim and I moved ourselves to the far side of the tent and invited in the students whose tent-erecting experience in the rain was an enormous failure. We didn't say anything; we didn't have to.

"I wish we had listened to you," said one young woman as she clutched her wet legs.

We all learned—late summer afternoons in Colorado are almost always wet with heavy monsoon rains.

Eventually, the rain stopped, and the long yellow rays of the crepuscular sun pierced the clouds. We emerged from the tent and shook the wet from our gear. As the students resumed setting up tents and spreading out their sleeping bags, I approached Juan's tent to let him know he could use my sleeping bag. I was more than a little surprised when I saw him pull a sleeping bag from his pack and spread it out.

"Juan, is that your bag?"

"No," Juan replied.

"We need to be sure you'll be warm tonight, so Mr. Jim and I have made a plan."

"I'm not sure what you are worried about," Juan replied. "I will sleep in this bag."

Confused, I said, "But you said you didn't have your bag."

"That's right. I don't have *my* bag. I borrowed my friend Mark's bag. Mark's not backpacking, so he didn't need it."

After two days hiking and two nights in our tents, we packed up our tents, cooking gear, and sleeping pads for the last time. We all sported a clear bounce in our steps as we approached the sixty-six-passenger yellow school bus—the starting point of our clockwise trail loop. A second group had arrived at the trailhead with us after travelling counterclockwise on the same loop, so our twenty students were joined by another set of twenty students and their two faculty leaders.

Jim and I took up the rear the last day, chatting and laughing. When we arrived at the bus, all forty students had released the straps of their packs and were reclining and recounting their adventures from the past three days. We connected with the other trip leaders and verified everyone was healthy—save for a few blisters—and the trips had gone well. We all were a little sunburned, smiling, and standing a little hunched with fatigue.

I was thinking of how Jim would drive the bus home after this trip while these kids slept in the back enjoying the heaters and not minding the firm seats and the smell of their bodies. I'd stay awake with Jim and the other adults, chatting to keep him alert as he drove the bus. The fine feeling of completing an exhausting trip was setting in.

Noting we'd need to drive out quickly to make it back to school before dark, I said, "Let's load up."

Then Jim said, "So, Jean, I need the keys to the bus. Keys please?"

"I don't have the keys, Jim."

He double-checked his own pockets, then unzipped the pouches on his pack. No keys to the school bus. As panic grew, we searched both of our packs together. No keys. We reviewed the trip; after three days of hiking, there was no telling where the keys had fallen. Even if we could get back to the camping sites, it would be a long shot to recover the keys.

The four faculty members moved apart from the students, out of earshot. In a tight circle, we began planning. How much food was left? I began a rationing process of food resources in my head. We had plenty of water. Who would hike out the twelve miles to town to make a call to school so we could be rescued? Where was the best place to start setting up tents before the afternoon monsoon began? The four of us were stressed and tired, and it showed. We were oblivious to the teens behind us, who clearly had noticed, recognized the problem, and decided to take matters into their own hands.

Just as we solidified how we'd proceed, we heard it. The sound was clearly someone revving the engine of an old four-on-the-floor school bus. All four trip leaders turned at once to see a senior student waving out the driver's window of the sixty-six-passenger yellow school bus grinning widely. He had hot-wired the bus.

Fly on the Wall

Fall 1988

How often do we say, "I'd like to be a fly on the wall when that happened?"

This moment in time defined me much like the dinner with Dr. Stone and Daisy, but in the opposite direction. During this moment, I was not even within fifty miles of the room. I can only play a fabrication of the scene in my head through a fly's eyes with details feeling surreal. I see the dust in the rays of the setting sun streaming through the large window facing the mountains to the west. I see the people in our meeting room, called in for an emergency meeting, eyes wide, watery, and alert as they leaned forward, hungry for every word spoken by the Head of School.

The setting was a small boarding school in the mountains of Colorado. The free and open spirit of the west kept the school alive and vibrant, but the funds flowing in certainly could not. We didn't hire subs for teachers; we covered for each other. While there was not a lot of money, there was a deep passion for kids, a love of seeing lightbulbs go off, and a belief we could make a difference in the lives of teenagers. I didn't know it yet, but the bug had already bitten me for this passionate and dedicated lifetime of service.

The day before this moment, I had called Dan, the Head of School, from the hospital in Denver. I tried to quit my job. I knew I couldn't teach for months, if ever again, and I knew the school couldn't afford a sub. He didn't accept my resignation.

"What will you do for health insurance?" he asked.

"I'll either be dead and will pass on 'bad debt' to the hospital, or I'll be psyched to be alive and declare bankruptcy." Having a large brain tumor helped me think rationally like this.

Dan's blue eyes looked down and he cleared his throat before addressing the people in the room. He is thirty-nine. I am twenty-six. Neither the fly nor I can understand, hear, or know how Dan tells these people my next few years would either be my last or be full of struggles, but I see my friends and colleagues leaning forward, soaking it all in.

When Dan asks, "What do we do?" Wendell's hand shoots up: "I'll take her third period class." Then Jim's, "I'll coach swimming." Then Leigh's, "I have no problem teaching another Geometry class," and so forth.

Even now, thirty-four years later, my chest tightens and my throat constricts when I think of these people in that moment who defined community, who defined the life I wanted to have, and who are my friends and ultimately my family for life by volunteering to do the job I could no longer do so I could retain health insurance and financial stability. Compassionate and committed, my friends and colleagues live as a community in a common human family. Like Australian Sheep Dogs, we round up each other lovingly, not wanting anyone to be left out of the circle.

Even though I loved teens, connected deeply with my colleagues, and felt a strong interest in teaching high school, I was still quietly reviewing the quote from the schoolteacher, Etta Pierce, in *Butch Cassidy and the Sundance Kid* about being in the bottom of the pit.

Except now, I edited the quote to include having a brain tumor. Clearly this was now a new low. Twenty-six, single, a schoolteacher, a brain tumor? Pulling myself up by the bootstraps, I committed myself to developing health and eventually walked to class with interest and passion, knowing this was, along with my beloved colleagues, all I had right now.

Transformation

Spring 1989

Still in the Cold War, I saw a bumper sticker in Colorado Springs: "RUSSIA SUCKS." As a former exchange student, I imagined if we could meet, know, and develop friendships with people in the Soviet Union, we might be able to move beyond the hatred. When glasnost policies began to open up the country, the USSR welcomed groups of students. Something in me clicked into high gear: *On it*.

Sometime after the paperwork, approvals, financial deposits, investments in the project, and the departure date was resolved, my doctors removed the brain tumor. The week before departure, I sat nervously in the neurosurgeon's office. "Do you think I could go?" I asked quietly.

"You can do whatever you want to do," he answered with a half-smile. "You know the risks." This was my third year teaching. I was still young and held the myth I was invincible. I would go.

Fast forward twelve days.

Our group clung together walking through the streets of beautiful Leningrad. I was tap-tapping my way with my one-point cane at the back of our group of students and teachers, collected tightly around our guide. It was 1989; we were behind the iron curtain. The Soviet government had confiscated our passports. Our IDs were simply "*visitkas*," which identified each of us by number and hotel. We had to carry our *visitka* on our person at all times; we turned it in at the hotel desk when we were in our rooms, and we collected it when we left. We had a strict nine p.m. curfew. Our movements were thus monitored. If we broke the rules, our departure from the country would thus be prevented.

I was aware I had my *visitka*, a few rubles, no language skills, and no knowledge of how to get from where I was to anywhere I'd like to go. We'd already had a student detained, one of us strip-searched, and film ripped from our cameras. We were not in Kansas anymore.

It was dark. The pathway under my feet turned to cobblestone. I was struggling to stay with the group. It was really cold; March in Leningrad is known for moist chill. The uneven cobblestones slowed me down, and I was beginning to focus intensely on where the group was headed. My headache pounded, collecting sharp pains around the incision scar on the left side of my skull. I could barely see my students and our guide. My visual field narrowed to a small tunnel, and my fatigue was not helping my balance and coordination challenges. My partial paralysis became more acute as I swung my left leg wide with each step. The group was further and further away, and I was working harder and harder to keep my students and colleagues in my sight. When I looked away from the cobblestones in their direction, I became dizzy and stopped to steady myself.

Now working to calm myself, I knew panic would only make things worse. My vision turned to a pinpoint. The stones under my feet seemed to sway. My cheeks were numb with the cold.

Then I felt a gentle hand on my right elbow, cupping the crook of my arm and raising me up to a fuller standing position, offering support. *Was I stooping? I must have been.* I tried to turn my head, but the world spun. Then I heard Jack's voice—Jack, the hockey player who threw the desk during my second day teaching. "I'll stay with you. Don't worry about keeping up with the group. We'll be fine." Jack was now a senior in high school; I was clinging to him for my life.

He escorted me, at my speed, until we met the group at our hotel. He was calm and continued talking to me slowly as my breathing was ragged and irregular. I couldn't turn to look at him. I couldn't speak. But I was calmed by his words and presence. It was only later when I quietly considered Jack's transition from a troubled ninth grader, barely positioning himself to arrive on time to class, into a confident senior, helping his injured math teacher navigate Nevsky Prospekt in Leningrad.

Teens have a fascinatingly serpentine and unpredictable growth pattern that captivates a close observer with the humor, challenge, and creativity of those young and developing minds. A young person turning a dark path into a bright path provokes a deep sense of awe. Teens have mind-blowing flexibility, adaptability, and growth potential. What other profession offers the opportunity to observe closely such a metamorphosis? What other profession allows a person to have a momentous impact on another? What other profession provides an extreme sense of responsibility, fun, satisfaction, and joy on a daily basis?

Grand Canyon

1990

It was a serious, multi-day backpacking trip into the Grand Canyon, and I was in charge of the adventure, along with my co-faculty member, Megan. Some of the young students were very skilled in wilderness activities, and some were new to camping in the outdoors. Megan was very experienced and well-respected by the teens. I was predominantly a math teacher who loved hiking. I was also only about a year post-operative and still experienced compromised coordination and balance.

Within the first day, it was well recognized that I, one of the trip "leaders," was the weakest backpacker in the group. While capable, I was slow and less certain on the rocks. I was last to arrive at the campsite and first to bed at night.

At the start of each day, everyone would get up on time, prepare, eat, and clean up after the morning meal, then assemble themselves, respectfully waiting for the morning "talk" about the expectations for the day. I was surprised these fine athletes and experienced outdoorspeople would pause to recognize Megan and me as leaders. Certainly, people of any age who are the most secure with themselves can also be the most humble.

The Grand Canyon. Even if you've never been there, the words tell you what it is—grand. Vishnu Temple towers above with painted layers of intricate patterns. If there's snow, which there was, then the upper layers are spread with a finely draped lace white tablecloth. Everywhere you turn, there's a new vision of color, shape, and glory.

But it's dry. We carry our own water—a gallon of water per person per day. Simply, the water makes for a heavy pack, never mind the clothes, sleeping bag, tent, cooking implements, and food.

On the first two days, I was hauling only half my share of water up the canyon wall, because one of the young and strong boys had said he wanted an "extra hard work out for basketball season" and volunteered to carry a gallon for me. Who was I to limit his athletic opportunity?

On the last day, I woke to feel deep fatigue. The students woke ready to climb. They assembled in the final circle as we discussed this last strenuous hike out of the canyon. Single file on a single track and very steep trail, I was second to last. Gregory, one of our two strongest and most experienced hikers, was behind me, chatty and pointing out the shapes around me with awe, joy, and positivity. I focused on not tumbling. He wore colorful reflective sunglasses and a big smile. My peripheral vision spun a bit with my balance challenges. The added focus required to pull myself up the last hill was exhausting. But I wasn't "in trouble." I was simply slow and labored. I was taking two steps forward and one step back every five or so seconds. Looking back now from twenty-five years away, I know Gregory could see what was happening and was committed to sticking with me.

About midmorning and halfway out of the canyon, Dylan, our other strongest hiker who had assumed a position near the front of our train, appeared before me, running down the trail towards me. Looking alert and wiry behind his wide grin, he said, "I'm taking your pack."

I contemplated the situation for a second. Dylan must have already climbed to the top, dropped his pack, and returned down to greet us.

"No, I'm good."

He tilted his head slightly to one side. "But you'd be better if I took your pack." At this point, I noticed Gregory and I were now far behind the group. Reluctantly, but admittedly with relief, I unclipped my chest and hip belts and slipped my shoulder straps down my arms. He adjusted the pack settings and shot me a grin and a questioning nod. "Ready?" And with that, he turned to lead me and Gregory up the trail.

Now sandwiched between our two strongest climbers and without my weight, I was elevated. I reached a foot up to a rock on the trail and was better able to lunge and stand on the forward foot. I was better able to look around at the shapes and colors Gregory observed. The lump in my throat had two sources—recognition that I was not as strong as I once was and recognition that these two fifteen-year-olds were taking care of me.

At the parking lot at the top, I sat. Rather, I collapsed into a sitting position. Then I reclined right on the tarmac, waiting for our van to pick us up. I was spent.

Driving back to campus, I recounted the day with Dylan and Gregory. Sheepishly, they admitted helping me was planned. They decided first Gregory would stick with me to verify I was okay and to take on extra weight if needed, and then Dylan would climb to the top as fast as he could, drop his pack, then return down to me and take my pack up the remaining part of the trail. They figured this was safest for the group. They also said they understood being a leader is not just being the fastest—and that to be a member of a group means you take responsibility for each member.

Seared in my memory is Gregory's young, grinning face and Dylan's crooked smile.

Not a Date

1991

"This is a perfect place to celebrate," Jim began. "There's hot springs at the top, lots of Columbine, Scarlet Gilia, and Daisy Fleabane this time of year, and enough snow to glissade down Triangle Pass." I was looking for a special walk in the mountains to celebrate the completion of my master's degree and had solicited Jim for both information and company.

Megan, who was a co-leader on the Grand Canyon adventure, would join us and provide great conversation. Jim would happily carry the tent. Jim's son, Paul, also had just finished his graduate degree and was looking for a celebratory backpacking adventure—it seemed obvious to include him. With several other colleagues and friends on the trip, I was ready and excited. I knew this would prove to be a memorable trip.

As the date of our adventure approached, other obligations required people beg out. My heart sunk with each change in plans.

"I'm sorry I can't join the group," one friend sadly said. "My mother's sick, and I need to stay close."

"Ugh. I can't believe my boss just scheduled this big meeting for that day," said another.

"Oh, man, Jean, I can't go this week—can we go next?" asked Megan. But I couldn't change the date.

Two days before our planned departure, only three people were left: Jim, Paul, and me.

Jim called on the phone, "I'm out, but you should go."

Paul and I were the two people celebrating completion of our respective graduate degrees and decided that we'd take his four-wheel-drive car the 250 miles to the trailhead.

"I have these great freeze-dried meals for camping," I volunteered.

"Not picky," replied Paul, quickly adding, "I'll bring the crackers, cheese, and a summer sausage." I had been camping enough with Paul's dad that I recognized the favorite lunch and snack items.

"I guess PB&J on tortillas for the first day on the trail goes without saying," I answered, raising an eyebrow. It was in that moment that I recognized we had both been trained in backpacking in Colorado by the same man, a man we both called "Dad."

We left the boarding school campus before dawn and were on the trail by eleven a.m. It was a ten mile hike up a couple thousand feet in altitude to the springs—we'd be there by dinner time. Our "before" picture shows us standing next to each other with the mountains behind us and a golden field of grass before us. Our clothes are clean and fresh and our smiles uncertain.

Two days and two nights later, we were singing our way down the trail, already reminiscing, and teasing each other about the cold-water stream crossing, the snow stuck in our jackets from glissading, and the fact that we repaired an injury creatively with moleskin because we both neglected to pack a first-aid kit. At the stream crossings, Paul reached out a hand instinctively to help me cross. He seemed to know exactly when my balance troubles surfaced in the same way he was able to apply medication into my eye damaged by the brain tumor.

During a quiet moment on the long walk down the valley, I felt elevated as I processed a thought I'd never had before: *I want to spend the rest of my life with this man.*

Our "after" photo shows us in the same field with the same mountains. Sporting a thin layer of dirt and big comfortable smiles, we are leaning against each other.

Leading with Compassion

1992

Strolling gently through the boarding school campus, I was evaluating the school as a place of prospective employment. Lush with the heat and humidity of central Texas and graced with limestone buildings, the school held a leadership position in the independent school world. I was enjoying the company of my host and feeling very good about the school and community there.

I was barely three years post-op from the large brain tumor and knew that I would not be able to drive a school bus, or any vehicle with students, because of my disabilities. Driving students was often a requirement of the job of a boarding schoolteacher. While I knew that legally I did not have to tell my interviewer, I still wanted to let him know my limitations. I did not want him to discover after hiring me that I would be unable to meet basic expectations.

With the athletic fields sprawling to my right and faculty housing to my left, I cautiously and slowly addressed Mr. Bennett. "Before we move any further forward, I would like you to know that I have some limitations that could be an important consideration."

His gate slowed, and he cocked his head. I had his full attention. "Three years ago, I had a large brain tumor removed. As a result, my hearing, vision, and balance have been impaired. I'm unable to drive students anywhere. I can't drive a school bus."

He stopped walking, turned, and looked at me with care and a touch of sadness. "That must have been hard for you."

His immediate, knee-jerk compassion took my breath away and was the beginning of a new journey at a school that I would embrace and that would embrace me back.

Fast forward two years. At the start of the summer, a terrible accident took the use of one of my students' legs from him. Paralyzed from the waist down and acutely aware of all he lost, Bart told his parents he wanted to return to his beloved school in Texas as a boarding student. His parents agreed that he might return to normalcy more quickly with his friends and in his community.

The problem? The school was not accessible.

In a meeting with the school administrators that included Mr. Bennett, Bart and his parents politely suggested that a ramp be put up in his dorm room and to one of the classroom buildings. The administrators looked at each other, puzzled.

"We will make all the buildings and facilities handicap accessible."

Construction began immediately, serving Bart his senior year and serving others in the years since.

Classy Pregnancy
1994

When my dream of a healthy pregnancy came true, I didn't tell them. I don't know why; maybe I thought it would be fun to see how teenagers acted when my body changes became increasingly obvious. Eventually, my abdomen grew into that awkward stage when no one can ask if you're pregnant because you might not be.

The room did become awkward, and I loved it. I could see the squirming and the whispers before class and chortled to myself. Students could barely pay attention.

One morning, while returning homework papers, I dropped the whole pile and about forty-five single pages filled with student scrawl fluttered in a five-foot radius around me. A dozen fifteen-year-olds leapt to their feet and scattered around me, collecting the papers, and looking up to me with begging eyes as they each handed me a pile. Those dear puppy dog eyes pierced my soul, and I started crying. Those young, beautiful, caring adolescents were showing big love in a way I had not seen before.

"Why are you crying, Ms. M.?" one young man asked.

I blurted, "Because you all are so wonderful, and I'm pregnant." Then I released a loud sob.

Some kids started clapping. Some kids jumped up and gave each other high fives saying, "Called it."

One boy wheeled a chair behind me, "Sit down and rest. Take care of your baby." The joy was palpable, which resulted in me crying harder. I realized that keeping this secret made the moment even more powerful.

During this and my other pregnancies, I was truly treated like a goddess by my students.

The school's religion teacher came to me one day and asked if I would receive his students in my office as a short "field trip." He explained his class was reading Eliade's *The Sacred and the Profane* and were discussing how to treat the sacred, in particular, the sacred earth. One student said, "You treat the earth like you would treat a pregnant woman."

"During their field trip to your office, would you let them touch your belly?" I was in my last trimester.

"That would be fine—through the fabric, of course?"

"Of course."

On the day of the field trip, the class lined up in front of me. One at a time, they either extended an index finger to poke or a flattened palm to feel my swollen abdomen. I juggled and slapped my side to see if I could wake up the fetus so they could feel movement. My son remained peaceful in there.

Then the last young man came forth, extended both hands, and cupped either side of my belly as if he were holding a sleeping baby. I was deeply calmed and thought this eighteen-year-old wise beyond his years. I watched him as he, still cupping my baby, lowered himself to belly button height and said, "Hello in there, Heeeelllloooooo."

Then a strong Braxton-Hicks contraction released itself in great fury, causing my flesh to go rigid and tight. Everett stepped back, wide-eyed, scared he had caused something bad to happen.

"No worries, Everett, " I said. "This is a Braxton-Hicks contraction."

He assumed a semi-squatting posture with his hands out to the side. "Contraction? I'll get the nurse. No, I'll call 911. Your husband? Shall I get your husband? Boil water? Do we boil water?" Everett was talking quickly. He was scared and wanted to be helpful.

I laughed, which did not seem to calm him. His classmates hovered around, nervous. I explained that my body was simply practicing labor, and I would not be delivering this baby in the next five minutes. His religion teacher chimed in with calming words of support.

Later that evening, I was warmed knowing these students experienced a meaningful lesson certainly beyond the normal school day. Many years later, I'm touched by a photo in the school's alumni magazine with a picture of Everett and his newborn son.

After my son was born, I returned to school with him to present him to the student body. The students—all four hundred of them—gathered in the chapel as I carried my son to the center of the church. Because the movie *The Lion King* had just been released, I planned to present my newborn in his best layette to the assembled student body in the same way Mufasa presented Simba.

With joy emanating from my face and body, I held my son up over my head with my arms extended. I rotated so all students could see his face. I thought him to be the most beautiful child I had ever seen. I was sure they would agree. The image of Simba being held high so all the animals of Africa could view his tiny frame was dominating my thoughts.

The students loved seeing the newborn. They cheered. Their cheers erupted into howls. *He must be blowing bubbles or doing something else super cute,* I thought. I walked left, then right, making sure everyone could see whatever wonderful thing he was doing. The howls became louder, the teenagers barely able to control their enthusiasm. I was a new, proud mother showing off her one-week-old baby.

My arms were getting tired, so I lowered him, pressing my son into my body. With horror, I realized that while I was holding him above my head, his diaper exploded, and runny baby excrement flowed freely down my arms and was now covering me and his best layette.

On my son's face was a look of complete satisfaction.

Colleagues who were also mothers flustered to my aid. The remaining colleagues ushered the now out-of-control student body out of the chapel.

I knew at that moment my son could never attend this school because he would never live this down.

The Great Sit

1994

Exiting the library, I inhaled slowly, enjoying the air of the late spring morning in Texas Hill Country. Because of the cloudless sky and the scent of freshly blossomed flowers, my pace was slow as I soaked in the clean air, the color green, and the pleasure of feeling bountiful. The path took me up the hill, past the chapel, and towards the limestone building which held my classroom.

The chapel on the hill had its doors opened, with white-robed chaplains ushering students and faculty into the building. This was unusual for this time of day. Even more unusual—adults I didn't know were gesturing towards the open doors, funneling all walkers into the cool stone building. The school was an arm of the Episcopalian Church. Every morning we gathered in assigned seats for morning prayers and music. The church building was a familiar and comfortable home, even for non-Episcopalians like me.

But this was not the start of the school day. We'd already had several class periods. I walked towards the transept to which my advisees and I were assigned, looking carefully at people's faces to determine the purpose of our surprise service. Everyone looked serious. The priests had started chants and liturgy which were unfamiliar to me.

I slipped quietly into a chair and placed my bookbag underneath. Sitting erect, I continued to search each person for some clue as to what was happening. My advisees slipped in beside me, quietly taking their seats and looking down, hunching their shoulders. No one was fidgeting. I was the only one looking around wanting to catch someone's eye.

With everyone assembled, the doors closed with soft thuds and the sanctuary became dark. I marveled that over four hundred bodies could be so still. The priests continued their chants.

This couldn't be good.

Many years later, I would be asked in an interview, "What was the greatest challenge you ever experienced in the field of education?" My answer to the interviewer was easy: "The death of a student."

The chants were the liturgy to mark a loss of life.

The hour inside the sanctuary was enough time for the school administrators to gather help. Counselors, members of the clergy, and a collection of other adults sorted through us as we left the church, pulling out those who appeared distraught. Afternoon classes were suspended for the day as faculty gathered with students, called parents, and made themselves available to anyone who needed someone. *Brilliant*, I thought. *These spiritual leaders have a recipe and program for healing.*

My interrupted walk was towards my Geometry class with a dozen tenth graders. The desks were arranged in an arc. Kevin's desk was the furthest to my left. I had just graded his homework. Earlier that morning, he had a headache significant enough for the school nurse to send him with his advisor to the emergency room of the local hospital. While waiting to be seen, he threw his arms back, fell backwards limply, and died.

"A congenital abnormality," they said. "No one could have predicted this or done anything about it."

The next day, at the same time of day, feeling not-quite-so-elated, I made the same slow walk. I was not carrying my books. I was not breathing as comfortably. I slowly opened the door to the classroom. The room was dark with the shades uncharacteristically drawn, but I could hear the breathing of eleven young bodies. I let my eyes adjust to the darkness to see one empty desk on the far side of the room to the left of my large teacher desk in front and eleven wide-eyed teenagers, crammed in their chair-desk combos on the opposite side, silently looking at me, wondering what we were going to do.

We sat quietly in the dark together with our own thoughts held tightly. I had to think of something. We couldn't stay here forever.

"May I turn on the lights? I really need to see your faces right now." I heard a murmur of agreement, so I turned on the lights.

"Let's stand in a circle." They moved the desks aside so there was a large empty space in the middle of the classroom.

No complaints.

"Closer. Get really close to your friend on your left and your friend on your right."

They complied.

"Rotate ninety degrees." I demonstrated, then stepped outside the circle.

"Take another step sideways towards the center of the circle."

Everyone stepped sideways. They were now belly-to-back.

"Do you trust me?" I asked.

They nodded.

"Do you trust each other?"

They nodded.

"Then sit on the knees of the person behind you."

Slowly, they lowered themselves onto the knees of the person behind them, thus offering up their own knees for the person in front of them. The circle was stable as they looked around, resting, and looking surprised.

"I call this the 'Great Sit.' I like this because we all need each other in order to be able to sit comfortably."

Soon, the circle dissolved, and eleven teens were on the floor, giggling, pushing, and poking each other.

I sat cross-legged on the floor with them, enjoying their return to the room. The giggling pink faces faded into quiet, sad faces.

One of Kevin's best friends spoke first. "I remember Kevin would always come a little late to this class because he had gym right beforehand, and they never quite gave us enough time to shower, but he always wanted to be sure he didn't stink."

"Yeah, the first time I saw him in this class, I thought his hair was greasy, but it was really just wet."

Then the flood began. "Remember when Kevin asked Minnie to the dance? He was such an old-fashioned gentleman with her! All us girls were jealous."

"The funniest thing happened in the dining hall last week—it was warm, and the windows were opened, and a sudden gust of wind blew the napkins out of the container all over the room. We all were scrambling to pick up the napkins blowing all over the place when Kevin immediately—and without even getting up—put a weight on top of the pile of napkins and stopped the problem. He had a way of seeing things."

"Remember the only day Kevin didn't do his homework? He always did his homework, and the one day he forgot, you gave a pop quiz."

"I appreciated how Kevin shared his notes from class with me when I was sick."

Exhausted, we became quiet again.

I let the students take the lead. One young man shifted the conversation. "You know, we are all really sad. I bet there's other people who are even more sad about Kevin."

I opened the desk and pulled out paper. Kids pulled out their pens and pencils and began writing to Kevin's parents, telling stories about fun times spent with him. Someone had colored pencils to share.

When they were done with writing their stories, drawing pictures, and sending heartfelt messages to Kevin's parents, I collected the papers and put the priceless collection in the mail.

I arrived early to school the next day and rearranged the desks and chairs in the classroom. I even moved the chalkboard. I put up new posters with affirming messages, with statements about friendship and kindness to others.

As I adjusted the room to prepare for my students' arrival, I began to understand one of the important lessons I was learning here. Founded and functioning in faith, the school had an inherent philosophy that we are here to serve each other. The students knew and lived it well—apparent in their beautiful transition from thinking about their own sadness to reaching out to Kevin's family members to offer them support and love.

God on Speed Dial

1994

We entered the canyon in Colorado at about one p.m. with a sliver of blue sky visible above the canyon walls. The student campers wanted to explore but were waiting for the okay from the trip leaders.

I took the lead. "Set up your tents. Put everything in your tents. Tie your flies tight and take your rain gear with you. Gather fire starters and store it under a tarp. Then go explore!" After many hikes in the southwest mountains, I knew the monsoons would open up the sky in midafternoon. Not only did I want my charges to be dry and comfortable, I wanted them to be safe.

My co-leader, less experienced in the outdoors of Colorado, looked at me, raising an eyebrow. The students whined, "Really? But Ms. M., the sky is blue! Everything is dry!"

I answered by setting up my own tent. Sometimes, there's no arguing with teenagers.

Then came the sarcasm. "Yeah, so when's it going to rain, Ms. M.? Next month sometime?"

I simply said, "3:00 p.m. to 3:30 p.m."

My supportive co-leader said, "You heard her. Do it before you go exploring the canyon." Being respectful students, they did as they were told. I wasn't going to ask them again.

Then we all ventured off to explore the rocks, plants, and river.

At 3:04, the rain started. It was no small rain. It was a downpour from the sky preventing you from breathing without holding your head down to create a cup of air. It was the kind of rain preventing you from seeing across the canyon to the wall fifty yards away. It was the kind of rain that made you run below whatever overhang you could find.

Then, at 3:30, the rain stopped. The clouds were cleared by 3:45.

The rest of the trip, I was treated like a goddess. They seemed sure I had a direct line to the weatherman in the sky. I pointed out I was, after all, incorrect about the start time of the rainstorm by four minutes.

"What's the temperature going to be tomorrow morning?"

"What time is the sunrise?"

Students let me sit in the best chair by the fire and served me dinner and breakfast. This was the best set of camping days ever.

"When will it rain today?" they inevitably asked.

"3:00 p.m. to 3:30 p.m." After the third day, they learned the afternoon monsoon weather pattern was very consistent. They also learned I would do my best to protect them and to care for them, even if I was not a conduit for divine messages.

I promptly lost my goddess status and had to get my own breakfast.

Lifelong Learning

Teaching adults is different from teaching adolescents. While my time teaching adults was short relative to the time I spent teaching adolescents, my adult students taught me humility, the power of motivation, and the importance of lifelong learning. These stories clearly show the powerful lessons taught to me by the people on the other side of the podium and demonstrate George Eliot's comment, "It's never too late to be who you may have been."

Fall 1998: I was an imposter, standing in front of sixty adults in a lecture hall. Unable to find a job teaching teens, I took a job teaching at a small state college in Colorado. Though the adult students, some of them over thirty, called me "professor," I felt like the high school math teacher I'd been for just over a decade. Usually, I looked out at fifteen squirrelly and ill-composed adolescents. Now, I looked out at serious adults, poised with paper and pencil ready for class to begin. Intimidated? You bet. I smoothed my blouse and arranged my notes on the podium.

A student raised her hand, "Professor?"

I looked behind me. Was there a professor behind me? *Oh no, she means me.* Would I ever get used to this?

Overwhelmed and red-faced, I can't remember what followed. I simply remember feeling out of place in my first several days as lecturer at a college. Mountain State was in the throes of transitioning from a two-year junior college to a four-year university.

Launching into the lesson, I moved swiftly—this was college, after all—until Sherry raised her hand.

"I'm lost. Could you start over?"

Flustered, I imagined pushing a reset button and began again.

These were not the kinds of students with whom I was familiar. These students ranged in age from nineteen to forty-five and were at school on their own accord, most of them funding their education themselves. There was no embarrassment at asking questions or making statements such as "I'm lost." There was simply a cold, hard, passionate desire to learn.

Later in my office with George, I explored who he was and how he landed at Mountain State College. "I'm thirty-five and have a son. I need to make more for a living than driving a pizza delivery truck is paying. That's why I'm here." I puffed out my cheeks, feeling the rawness of his emotions and sense of urgency and insecurity. "My goal is a real job. I want to be a professional...something. Just something to help me take better care of my family."

Robin joined me later. Her body's shape revealed a single mastectomy. At the time, it was the culture in our small town to refuse reconstructive surgery after a mastectomy. "Here I am at age thirty, starting my life over after cancer. My dad doesn't think I can earn any grade better than a C. I'm going to prove him wrong. I want to be a scientist and contribute to our understanding of cancer."

Then, Susan: "You can't fail me. I need to learn this. I need to graduate so my children have a role model." Susan sat front and center and was outspoken about what she understood and what she didn't understand. This helped make my job easier. I could immediately address her needs, and in doing so, everyone was helped.

Teaching adults proved to be a very different ball game from teaching high schoolers. These people understood more of the "real world" and the difference an education could make in their lives. They carried within a fierce desire to make their world better, in many cases, better for their children. They wanted to be parents of proud children instead of children of proud parents.

Sometimes the only difference between teachers and students is who holds the keys to the room and the chalk for the blackboard. Everyone is learning. Everyone is insecure. Everyone feels like an imposter; George and I both wondered if we belonged in the room.

Spring 1999: "Bonus time!" I said two weeks into my first teaching gig at Mountain State College and fifteen minutes before the end of class. I taught a class with students that had failed the most basic math placement test and were starting at stage one: Pre-Algebra and Algebra, which I rolled into one basic course.

When I looked out at the sixty faces, I could see an "alert" expression.

"At the end of each class, I'll explore extensions or applications of the ideas we've been studying. These ideas will appear in future math classes. This will give you a jump ahead and make your next math class just a little easier."

The pizza delivery man, George, pursed his lips and nodded his head.

"You will not be tested on this material. I'm just showing you some fun and cool things appearing down the road, should you choose to take more math."

We had been studying the quadratic formula and the concept of conjugates with real numbers. At least a few students thought it was "cool" that an irrational number multiplied by its conjugate becomes rational. The next level topic I chose to address with them during our bonus time was imaginary numbers. The "square root of negative one" was not something anyone in the room felt comfortable with, but they still allowed me to continue and to show conjugates of imaginary numbers and the complex plane. I graphed complex numbers, then powers of complex numbers. While this seemed a little over some students' heads, I thought if even one student grasped this or later found their lives easier, then the time was worth it.

George thought the spiral created by powers of complex numbers was one of the coolest things he'd ever seen. He stayed after class, asking questions, pushing my own academic limits.

Fast forward a year. I ran into George in the hallway. "Professor," he started.

I cringed at the title. "Call me Jean, please."

"Jean," now he cringed, but he continued, "I couldn't stop thinking about those extra bonus topics you'd introduced to us last year. Then I retook the placement test in mathematics and ended up placing out of the next two courses. I'm now well on my way to being a math major, even though math scared the willies out of me last year. But what I really learned is that I could be anything I wanted to be. No subject scares me anymore. I just wanted to say thank you."

I congratulated him and wished him well. My steps were light walking down the hall.

Several days later, I ran into Mike, from the same class but only twenty years old. "Professor," he grinned. I couldn't correct him because he spoke quickly.

"After our course, I retook the placement test because I heard George had done well after our class. I placed out of the next two math classes."

My jaw dropped.

"But I decided to take each of those classes anyway because I don't want to miss any small idea. I simply love math. Thank you."

If my teaching career had ended then, I would have been satisfied I had made a difference. More than anything else, however, was the humility I felt by the efforts, interest, and motivation of these people who had previously categorized themselves as unable to "do" math. I'd had academic support and encouragement my whole life—these people had not. They were making themselves into better people, catapulting themselves into a new and better life that might include owning and managing the pizza establishment for which they once drove a truck.

Spring 1999: "I can't teach her," I told the dean through the clunky school phone. "Mae can't speak English." He was silent.

"I know we have an admission standard," I continued. "People must score at least a fifty on the TOEFL (Test of English as a Foreign Language). I'm sure she didn't do well enough on the TOEFL to attend school here." I was frustrated with trying to teach the language of numbers to someone with whom I shared no common vocabulary.

"We thought it a good match," said the dean. "Do your best."

I hung up the phone and thought of my student. Mae was Asian, quiet, and looked lost. I couldn't assign an age to her; there was a timelessness about her skin, expression, and slender body covered with oversized clothing. At times she seemed old, maybe fifty, and there were times she was so timid I thought she was a teenager. I knew I needed to pull up my bootstraps, get to know her, and do my best to teach her math.

The next day, I insisted she come to my office. "I want to help you with the math," I said.

Later in the day, Mae shuffled into my office, holding her math book and spiral close to her belly and looking down at her hands clenching her books. I gestured towards the chair in my office.

"Can you tell me about yourself?" I wanted to know her story. I wanted to see what words she understood so I could use those. I needed to see what words I needed to teach her for us to be successful. I needed to see she was motivated. In our first meeting, I pulled out every ounce of patience I could muster.

"Where are you from?" I pulled out a map. Mae pointed to Cambodia, then moved her finger towards Viet Nam. "How did you make it here?"

"My sponsor. I have a sponsor."

The idea that this young Cambodian woman suddenly landed in small-town western Colorado was astonishing.

"So, let's do some math." We started with symbols. She had never seen an equal sign, so I started with that. When I could handle no more, she was still wide-eyed and sitting at the edge of her chair. There was an excitement in her venture beyond even the enthusiasm of George, the thirty-five-year-old man who didn't want to drive pizza delivery trucks all his life. The light behind her eyes inspired me. She had a hope, an inspiration, and a drive I found powerful.

Her English improved over the course of the semester, certainly more swiftly than I had expected. "So, tell me about yourself," I asked again, after we'd been working together a couple months.

"I was young, about ten, when I saw my mother and older brothers killed in the center of my town by Pol Pot's regime."

I was aghast. My mind raced as my jaw dropped. *Pol Pot? Mae must be almost forty, about my age.*

"My father grabbed me, and we ran." She looked at me to gauge my reaction. I tried not to look as horrified as I felt. "We ran at night and slept during the day until we came to the border of Viet Nam, where we ended up in a refugee camp. We lived in a tent village. There was no school there. Many people were sick and hungry."

I felt an upwelling inside for this woman. I was in my seventh month of my second pregnancy and my hormones were surging, making me feel a heaviness in my heart and soul. I would help her. I had to help her.

I found some relief in returning to mathematics. Later, her story would revisit my consciousness. I could not escape visions of what her life had been like in Viet Nam and Cambodia, as she couldn't escape her life experiences. She was a quick and motivated learner. She had an ability to think abstractly and moved swiftly from arithmetic to algebra.

She would appear in my office hours twice each week, ready to move herself forward in math. I would milk her for a little more of her story each time.

"One day," she shared with me while looking at my swollen belly, "a pregnant woman ran into my tent screaming. Her baby was coming." She swallowed hard. "I was twelve. I hadn't even had my first period yet." She looked up at me, sharing a story that must have changed her life. "I delivered the baby."

"How did you know how to deliver a baby?"

"I didn't know. I just followed my..." she tapped on her sternum lightly. "I didn't have a choice; the baby was coming."

"What were you thinking at the time? What were you feeling?"

"I was scared. I didn't understand all the water—it burst out and hit me in the face, and I was surprised by the salty taste. But the baby was healthy, and the mom also did very well."

She was clearly very proud of the successful delivery.

"Then people heard I delivered a healthy baby, so all the women wanted me to help them with their babies. When I was fifteen, I knew how babies were born so well I could help people—really help people—deliver their babies. And I learned how to stay out of the way of the water."

Mae had learned a valuable skill. Not a skill you'd really want to learn on-the-job as she had, but she was all anyone had there in the refugee camp on the border of Cambodia and Viet Nam.

I looked at her now with awe and respect. I marveled at her journey of survival. "So, you could deliver my baby?"

She laughed, "Yes, but you don't want me. You want an American doctor."

"How many babies have you delivered?" I was curious now. She just shrugged. "Over a hundred? Over two hundred? Over five hundred?" I guessed.

She shrugged again. "Many, many babies. About fifteen years' worth of babies. Then my sponsor found me. She was working in my camp with the Red Cross and thought I needed better training, so I'm here to become a nurse so I can go back and help my people."

Mae passed the class with flying colors. I saw her last just before her graduation. I imagine now she's been a nurse in Cambodia or Viet Nam for two decades, delivering babies, saving lives, and serving her people with an extraordinary instinct, natural skill, and with an education to support her through the more difficult deliveries.

Whenever some of my high school students needed perspective, I share her story. Indeed, whenever I need perspective on my own life, I consider her story.

Part 4: Cruising

"Teaching is not a job. It's a lifestyle. It permeates your whole life."

– Dr. Jill Biden

After about the third year in a classroom, one school year starts to bleed into the next; one school experience bleeds into another. Student faces often merge, stories fade or become more colorful with retelling. The teacher, parents, and students have greater faith in the teacher's skills, allowing for more fun experimentation and classroom adventures.

After teaching a few years, my world changed. Everywhere I looked, I saw something I could use in the classroom. Every new experience was something to share with students. My world was defined in terms of how I could use what I saw with my students. A medical crisis had revealed the true character of my colleagues and led me to understand this life immersed in high school education was for me.

A parent of a former student astutely observed, "You're like Jimi Hendrix who used to sleep with his guitar." I began to cruise into the flow, the music, and the delight of a life in education.

Ambition

1991-2001

"The person we have in mind for the job is further along on his master's degree, has more classroom experience, and is, quite frankly, older than you," Patrick said, tipping his head to the side with a faint smile. His elbows rested on his desk, supporting his gently folded hands just below his chin.

I was prepared for this question and for this job. I'd been teaching for five years, and my master's degree was nearly complete. I wanted to be math department chair. I knew how to respond.

"The dean of the school hasn't started his master's. The English department chair*man* is younger than I am and has fewer years in the classroom." I swallowed hard but kept my eyes locked on his. "If there's a difference, then I need to know so I can address my weaknesses and prepare myself better. If there's not a difference, then you need to know."

Patrick's face paled as he spoke in a deep monotone. "This is not a gender issue."

"I didn't say it was." It was my turn to smile.

A quick, efficient, and pointed response rarely presents itself in my mind; this was a rare gem.

In the early spring of 1991, I was the first woman at that school granted a contract that included the words "department chair." Another female teacher would later sign a similar contract as Spanish department chair. In about five months, the two of us were the first women to serve on the Academic Committee as chairs, not chairmen, of our academic departments. Our appointments heralded a new chapter in the life of the school.

During my first tenure as a department chair, I discovered though I loved curriculum development, aiding in the professional development of my department colleagues, and helping to guide the school on an academic path, the other obligations were less pleasant to me and simply took away my valuable and fun time in the classroom. I learned I simply enjoyed teenage energy and wanted to spend time with teenagers, turning on lightbulbs, giving confidence and skills, and reaping the benefits of being a part of rapidly developing minds and psyches.

Two years later, I reluctantly assumed the position of department chair at a different school, where there were many highly revered female department heads. Resetting the math curriculum and working with the wonderful faculty members there was satisfying, but my experience reinforced that my interests lay in helping young people move along successfully at the start of their life journey. My ambition evolved into becoming the best teacher I could be, developing lessons that encourage young minds to appreciate and enjoy learning, and connecting with teens as they navigated the challenges of high school. I used math teaching, coaching, and outdoor activities as the vehicle for these connections.

So, when I sat in yet another interview for a teaching position in 2001, I was clear with myself what I was in the market for—a job I loved teaching ninth, tenth, eleventh, and twelfth graders. *Not* department chair, which apparently was open.

"Are you interested in department chair?" Len, the Assistant Head of School, asked. This was a role I had in 1991, and I knew myself better now.

"No, I'm a classroom teacher." In a world where teaching is a lower-paying job held mostly by women, and school administration is a higher-paying job held mostly by men, I was pained to fall in step with a traditionally feminine role and accept lower pay.

Len was slumping in the chair, as he was known to do, with his chin thrust slightly forward, looking at me through the bottom of his glasses, "So you're not ambitious."

This was not one of those times when I had a turn of phrase ready. I was not prepared for any school administrator calling a career classroom teacher unambitious. His comment caused me pause. In his world, working towards excellence in a feminine job is not ambitious; moving towards a masculine job is ambitious.

In the years since, I've replayed the moment in this interview, practicing what I'd say if I ever encountered a similar comment. "Oh my," I'd say, "my ambitions are far greater than department chair. My great ambition lies with helping students grow to love math and become capable mathematicians with a plethora of options available for their career choices," or "My ambition lies with educating young people to become their best selves in and out of the classroom," or "My goals exceed a chair position; my goals include creating lessons drawing in my charges to the joy of mathematics and the love of problem solving," or even, "I'd like to focus on my teaching and the more meaningful job of connecting with students."

I developed a harder shell as the interview progressed. Len continued, "I find math teachers develop a set of lessons, then simply repeat them over the years because they are lazy, and the field doesn't change. Math has stayed the same for decades."

I was ready for this one. "But, oh, high school math is very different now than it was ten years ago. Calculator technology has allowed topics previously covered only in college courses to be included in the high school curriculum, causing math programs to adjust the standard curriculum dramatically. For example, regression analysis is now a standard high school topic, when just ten years ago it was covered only in college statistics classes." He raised an eyebrow but had a look of skepticism.

I went further. Knowing he was a part-time administrator and part-time English teacher, it was again my turn to smile: "There's a parallel with English literature. Do you teach Shakespeare?"

Ancient Mandarin

2001

Lin humbled me. She had no single first language; she learned English, Spanish, Cantonese, and Mandarin from birth, as her parents spoke all these languages in her home equally. Her goal was to finish high school fluent in eight languages. As a high school junior, she was well on her way to achieving her goal.

At the time she applied to our school, she was living with her family in South America and stated on her application her language of choice was Spanish. She also identified herself as "Lina." Greeting her on the first day in the dorm, I was surprised to see she was Taiwanese and not Latina or Hispanic. She flowed comfortably between and around different cultures. I marveled at hearing her speak to parents in sentences containing words from a multitude of languages, all with accents displaying her fluency with each. It was my joy to know young people with such skills. Sometimes this job simply kept me humble.

Looking through a clothing catalogue one day, I saw a well-endowed model wearing a yoga t-shirt with a Chinese character on it. I didn't know if it was Mandarin or Cantonese, but Lin knew both those languages. The catalogue advertised the symbol meant "peace," and I intended to use my knowledge to connect with Lin and to impress her with my international sensibilities. With international tensions threatening escalation, it seemed touching, moving, and appropriate to write "peace" on the board in a different language each day for one week. My idea was to start with the Chinese symbol from the magazine, then move to the Latin "pax" the next day, then the Russian "mir" after, and so forth.

On the day I wrote the Chinese character on the board, I wore a pair of red pants adorned with Chinese characters. I felt international.

But Lin said nothing and had no response. After class, I asked her if she'd noticed the character.

"Yes," she said and looked a little confused.

I pulled out the catalogue and showed her the image. She bent over in a full belly laugh, and with tears spilling down her face, she explained the 38-D model smiling glamorously was wearing a shirt imprinted "flat."

"My pants, Lin, my pants? What do they say?" I was prepared for anything.

She dried her tears and became contemplative. "It took me most of the class period to recognize the character. It's Ancient Mandarin and if you reverse the character and turn it right-side up, then it best translates to 'dragon.' Now as I look more closely, some characters are just upside down, some are rotated ninety degrees, and some are upright. It's a mishmash."

I was crushed.

"You could say it's either good, backward, or backward both ways," she added with a shrug and a smile.

This somehow seemed appropriate.

I had to wrap my mind around the fact that she also knew Ancient Mandarin and could perform a composition of transformations in her head.

More than just marveling at her skill, I cringed at my inability to remember the most basic consideration while doing research—I failed to consider my source of information. I had to forgive myself and realize you're never too experienced to make a rookie mistake.

Back at the Salida ER

2003

The ambulance was weaving swiftly down the canyon road from Monarch Ski Area towards Salida, Colorado. Tammy was with me in a cervical brace and her full body was restrained to stabilize her. The paramedic was monitoring her vitals. I pulled out my cell phone and tried to call her mom or dad.

"Kay? Is that you?" The connection was poor and wobbly. Kay lived in Pueblo, Colorado, just east of the mountains. She was roughly an hour out of Salida, but on the other side of the small town from us.

"Yes, who's this?"

"Jean Mariner here. Tammy took a fall on the ski slope, so we are headed to the Salida Hospital in an ambulance. I thought you might want to join us there." I was sitting on a hard bench next to Tammy, my body swaying in synchrony with the curves in the road.

"Sorry, I can't hear you?"

With every turn, we either came into cell service or out. Kay didn't have a cell phone, so texting was not an option.

"Tammy. Fall. Salida Hospital. Meet us." I repeated the sentence fragments several times slowly, thinking she'd catch most of it. I could hear her apparently better than she could hear me. I had met her once at drop-off day but had long learned while I didn't remember each parent, each parent remembered me well. My conversational tone with Kay was one of a peer, a friend, and a person who cared about Tammy. I could not conjure an image of Kay, but that wasn't relevant. At forty-one, I could handle an ambulance ride and this conversation better than at twenty-three, when I started teaching.

In the seventeen years since the failed ER conversation with Fern's mom, and about fifteen years since my self-absorbed reaction to Mark's broken arm, so much had changed for me. I was more effective with parents, even when I felt as though I was exploding on the inside. I was more emotionally connected to the young people I spent my time with in the classroom, dorm, and during weekend activities. I understood each of them was someone's son or daughter and was deeply loved because now I had my own children.

Here, now, headed to Salida with Tammy, my affect expelled calm, but my insides were completely out-of-control. My throat was constricted, my eyes were welling up, my nose was running, and my chest was shaking.

"Kay, I'm with her, holding her hand. It's a possible head and neck injury." It was all I could say because of the constriction in my throat. Tammy is her baby.

"No, no, no!" screamed Kay. "I'm on my way."

"Kay, wait. I'm going to put the phone next to her ear. Can you talk with her?"

"Yes."

I know the shaking in my chest was mirroring hers as I put the phone next to Tammy's left ear. "Hi, Mom," Tammy said softly. "I'm okay."

I couldn't hold myself in. "Tell her you can wiggle your fingers and toes."

"Mama? I can wiggle my fingers and toes."

I could verify this by how she pressed her fingers into mine.

"Mama, yes, I can wiggle my fingers and toes." Kay couldn't hear. The connection was still wobbly as the ambulance stayed in the track of the serpentine road.

Then Tammy closed her eyes. "I can't talk anymore."

I took the phone and said, "She can wiggle her fingers. And toes. Meet us there. I'll stay with her until we see you."

"What? She can wiggle what?"

"Her fingers and toes."

"Thank God." Then the phone went dead.

Tammy was a sophomore in one of my algebra classes. Always bubbly, yet sensible in her approach to school, she attended boarding school because her family owned and worked a rural Colorado cattle ranch. She was a clear-skinned, flowing-haired, apple-cheeked, bareback horseback rider, who laughed hard and knew how to connect with people as well as she could connect with her horses. As we followed the serpentine road down the canyon, I saw in my mind's eye Tammy chewing on her pencil as she took a math test and sailing through the air on her horse. I imagined her moving freely and sporting a wide and bright grin. I saw her playing with blocks on the floor when she babysat my own children.

Kay met us in the ER at nearly perfect timing. She and Tammy disappeared in the back recesses of the building, leaving me alone in the waiting room with Tammy's health forms clenched in my fist, now no longer needed because Tammy's parent was there.

I sat in the squeaky Naugahyde seats in the drafty waiting room as the sun cast orange light on the walls. I paced around the array of chairs in the empty waiting room, wondering when I might hear what was happening. The streetlights clicked on as dusk descended. I sat again, only to get up to walk around a few minutes later.

Then Tammy and Kay emerged, Kay's arm around Tammy as she walked slowly. Kay looked up at me and smiled, "All tests were negative. She can go home and rest." I kissed Tammy on the forehead and watched the two of them walk slowly to the truck advertising their ranch.

I picked at my cuticles as I slouched in the Naugahyde chairs until someone from school picked me up.

Are We Ever Going to Use This?

2007

The jobs current students will have throughout their lives don't exist today. Some jobs are so far beyond our imagination, we can't even fathom what specific techniques or skills students will need. The best set of skills a young person can develop in this new millennium includes creativity, problem solving, communication, and the ability to research effectively. Technology was evolving fast in the 1980s and 1990s—so fast we could not see where the world would be in ten years.

Brad was a junior in 1986. Really smart and driven by the practical, he sat in the back row, leaning back. The chair was attached to the desk, making the desk rise to the seated student's chin level. This drove me nuts, as I always imagined the chair-desk combo slipping, causing bleeding or broken bones for the student leaning back. One firm look from me and Brad returned the desk to the floor.

"I'm serious, Ms. M., what good is this? How does it move us forward? We just spent forty-five minutes drawing a flower. I can't get back that wasted time." He scoffed.

I just spent forty-five minutes working with students to graph a rose curve with eight petals, using polar graphing, major angle trig function values, and a variety of symmetries. Our reward was an image of a daisy on a polar grid. I was standing back, looking at the board, admiring the class's work. The year 1986 was just prior to Texas Instruments and other companies marketing calculators able to graph the same flower in a matter of seconds, allowing students to take the analysis of polar graphing to a new level. All we had now was our wits, our patience, and our skills.

"But Brad, isn't it simply beautiful? Isn't it cool we can do this?" I'm sure I had an ear-to-ear grin plastered on my face. This was genuinely beautiful math, a spirograph from my youth.

He emitted a sound best described as a snort.

Ten years later, the graphing and programmable calculator is a staple in the math classroom. The internet is blossoming into an indispensable tool for companies, educators, and anyone who wants to communicate. The same rose curve can be graphed on the calculator in a manner of seconds. It's a new world.

Brad approached me during his twenty-year reunion celebration. "Uh, Ms. M.? I'm just wondering if you remember the day we used polar graphing to create a rose curve?"

"Yes, Brad, I do."

He then described how he used the qualities of polar graphing to create an analog clock on a web page he was designing for his job. While impressed he used a concept from his high school math class in his post-graduate job, I was more impressed he had found a novel use for the polar graphing technique he had found so objectionable in 1986, because he saw no application at the time.

He had found an application.

For each year following, when a student asked, "When are we ever going to use this?" I replied, "That's for you to find out," and I tell the story of how Brad learned about polar graphing when the internet was barely a twinkle in the eye of a developer, yet Brad was able to apply polar graphing in a way no one had ever previously imagined.

Ms. Peach

2008

"Listening to wisdom can change your life," I said the first day in class. "You never know when or where wisdom will occur for you. Your assignment tonight is to read a piece that's personal to me and to respond in your own math blog."

Confused that this math class will begin with a writing assignment, they shrugged. Usually the first day, a teacher can ask students to do nearly anything, and they will comply. The first two days are a honeymoon. In our honeymoon, I wanted to set a tone of open-mindedness and learning.

That night, they read:

> In the late twentieth century, my family lived in Grand Junction, Colorado, at the juncture of the Grand and Colorado Rivers. Just east of town is the town of Palisade, famous for peaches. Just west of town is the aptly named town of Fruita.
>
> Our rental house, about 1,500 square feet of damp stucco and thin pine floorboards from the 1920s, sported a flower garden. When I moved in, I didn't pay much attention to plants; after all, I killed most of the houseplants I had ever owned. First bloomed the Peonies. Each large, lacy, fluffy, light-pink billow was so fragrant, the scent of one in a simple spherical bowl would fill the house. Different flowers bloomed in succession until the roses, the many roses, bloomed. The wiry and pokey stalks of plumes spread across the yard in wild wonder, blissfully taking over the play area.
>
> Our neighbor, Barbara, a proud nonagenarian, leaned over the fence. "I have some clippers you could borrow for those rose bushes," she said. I smiled, knowing if I did anything to these plants then they would surely not survive.

One morning, I found the clippers and some gloves on a table in our backyard. I began using the clippers more like a scythe on the rose bushes so the size of our yard would be increased, allowing for more play space. Later in the day, I returned the clippers to Barbara and thanked her. She smiled and gently said, "You know, if you cut the roses at a forty-five-degree angle five leaves below the last bloom, then your roses will blossom again."

I smiled back, knowing I could not have cared less about the roses.

It was only two weeks later when I found myself cutting the roses as she had recommended, and not even a month later when our world became filled with Elizabeth, Sunrise, Blood Orange, and Pink Beauty roses. Our yard was beautiful. I took great pleasure in gifting friends bouquets of roses and in decorating our home with fresh-cut roses.

And so it went with peaches. Bushels appeared on my porch from well-meaning friends. "Surplus," they said, "from the orchards in Palisade and Fruita. Can them." I smiled, knowing I didn't like peaches and liked cooking even less. Clearly, the peaches would rot. Barbara said canning was easy. "Would you like to borrow my pot for a try? I have some extra pectin and can show you an easy technique for removing the skin."

It was barely ten days before the lids of my first set of Jammin' Peaches began making friendly popping noises, signaling a tight seal as the peaches cooled inside the pint glass jars.

Each summer since then, I've canned fruits of the fields. Peaches, blueberries, blackberries, nectarines, prickly pears, cherries, apricots. I've canned a rich chocolate syrup for ice cream. I love all parts of this food preparation process: the feel of the berries on my fingers, the swell and smell of the bubbling syrup around the stainless-steel spoon, the sound of the cooked and sweetened fruit slipping into the jar, and of course, the popping lids. I've tested and savored different flavors in my preserves: lime, lemon, lavender, basil, almond, vanilla, and have kept a long list of my recipe experiments in my thick book on canning. It's been well over twenty years since Barbara handed me her shears, her pots, and her wisdom, but I think of her with every batch I boil. Listening to her wisdom changed my life.

The student responses were priceless and mostly on target. "I think you want me to ignore the fact I hate math. But I've always hated math."

And, "I get it. You want me to try new things because I may like it."

And, of course, "Can you bring in some chocolate syrup or peach jam for us? We can have a party. How about peach pie? Ice cream?"

Bathroom Break

2009

He was regular, I'll say that.

As an eighth grader, at precisely 9:14 a.m. every day, he needed to use the bathroom. This happened even if I was in the middle of a hopefully captivating lesson, giving a quiz or test, or even if a peer was explaining a solution on the board. Even if he, himself, was involved in addressing a classroom exercise. He'd raise his hand, announce his need, and even writhe a little to demonstrate. No, he couldn't wait.

One day we chatted after class. "Let's plan to have you use the restroom before class begins, so you don't interrupt the flow of the lesson." He agreed, but still, at 9:14, he had to go.

Clearly, this was atypical for a fourteen-year-old male. I began to be concerned. I phoned home. "Mr. Jacobs? I'm concerned about Tony's health." I explained the trouble and my concern there may be a medical issue. In the back of my mind lurked the possibilities: a urinary tract infection, bowel inflammatory disease, or worse. The father expressed appreciation for the heads up. He called me back the next day and explained that math caused his son anxiety, and this anxiety "kind of got things going for him."

I noted the 9:14 observation in the required comments at the end of each grading period and alerted the school nurse.

I had the good fortune of having him in math class the same period of the day three years later. He remained just as regular as an eleventh grader. But this bathroom habit didn't start until the second week of classes.

"Yes, Ms. Mariner, it's the same issue—anxiety," Tony said as he looked down.

Right, I thought. I called the parents and discussed how this might be an issue during tests or down the road in college. "Perhaps our school counselor could help or make a recommendation?" They'd follow up with their son, they said.

Shortly thereafter, one of my colleagues was in the boy's restroom and found Tony with a collection of plastic bags, each with a rectangular solid appearing to be a brownie. He was selling them for twenty dollars each. The faculty member gathered the marijuana-laced brownie collection and escorted Tony to the dean's office.

I never saw Tony again. The school officials determined Tony began his "work" as an "entrepreneur" in eighth grade, noting my 9:14 a.m. observations in my comments at each grading period.

The interesting part of my experience with Tony was how it affected me. Surely, I was sad for him and what this meant, but now every time a student needed to use the restroom, an alarm went off inside my head. Was this young person dealing drugs? Several years after Tony would have graduated, I told this story to my classes and revealed to them each time they went to the restroom, I was suspicious and scared for them. Tony's behavior had colored me so much, it was affecting how I responded to current students needing to use the restroom.

The result? Students stopped taking bathroom breaks. They planned ahead or waited.

Occasionally, someone would need to use the restroom and would gingerly raise a hand. "Ms. Mariner, may I go deal drugs?"

"No, you may not," I'd respond. "But you may be excused to use the bathroom."

Mouse in the House

Fall 2010

Late one evening, while grading papers, I saw a small rodent skit across our living room. I set up traps—sixteen of them—all over the room to catch the little guy and his buddies.

In the morning, I gingerly checked all the traps—no mouse, cheese still there. I left for school thinking we would certainly see the traps snapped by the time we came home in the afternoon.

At about 10:30 a.m., just after a fifteen-minute break for students to gather books and run around outside a bit, there was an announcement on the intercom. A mouse had been discovered in the sophomore commons. The custodial staff and administration repeated the rule, "No food in the commons or classrooms," and explained that a mouse, though dead, had been discovered.

I thought, *Wow, I guess it's getting cold enough outside for these critters to venture indoors.*

When I returned home, the mouse traps in our home were still set with cheese. No mouse. I was in the process of setting up more when my son spoke from the kitchen.

"Ah, Mom? No need to set the traps. I got the mouse."

I looked him up and down, from his scuffed hair down to his peanut butter and jelly to his size fourteen running shoes. "You caught the mouse? How?" I asked, wide-eyed.

He shrugged and took another bite of his sandwich. "He slept in my shoe last night."

"And?" I waited.

He quietly chewed. "And what?" It seemed clear he did not want to share more.

I nodded a little, raising an eyebrow to encourage more information.

"He was so little! I thought I was flattening lint in the toe of my shoe." He looked nauseated and put down his sandwich.

"I got lucky no one was looking when I took off my shoe in the commons this morning."

"During the 10:30 break?"

"Yeah. I'd been stretching and wiggling my toes in what I thought was lint for about three hours." He shoveled his half-eaten peanut butter and jelly sandwich into the trash.

I stared at him in disbelief for not knowing there was a mouse in his shoe and for not finishing his sandwich.

"Not hungry anymore."

He made me swear I wouldn't tell anyone. So, I didn't.

The following year, just as the weather was becoming chilly, the administration made an announcement. "Do not bring food into the classroom building. Last year, we had a mouse in the sophomore commons..." It was all I could do not to guffaw, but I never told the origin of the dead mouse.

The year after *that*, also as the weather was becoming chilly, the same announcement was made, "A mouse was found in the sophomore commons a short while back..."

This continued each fall, all ten years I taught at that school following the mouse incident. Everyone was very serious about the rodent intruders, except my children and me, who hid our chuckles when the announcement was made.

I'm sure the "no food" policy and the fear of mice helped the custodial staff immensely in their efforts to keep the building clean. I like to think my son's size fourteeners did an enormous public service.

When You Least Expect It

2012

"I bet you each a dollar you will forget this next way of proving triangles congruent."

"No way!" they all answered enthusiastically. They didn't realize I meant the bet was on for more than one year.

First-year high school students were in a yearlong geometry course studying the methods of proving triangles congruent. There is an element of redundancy to the methods taught: Side-Angle-Side, Side-Side-Side, Angle-Side-Angle, and Angle-Angle-Side. These are abbreviated, for example, S-A-S refers to Side-Angle-Side.

The list above excludes another method of demonstrating the uniqueness of a triangle or congruence of triangles. Hypotenuse-Leg falls in a different pattern; H-L deviates from the S and A patterns of the other methods, so it's often forgotten.

But once I said, "I bet..." and "you will forget..." the game was on and every fifteen-year-old was programmed to win. For the rest of the year, every time I asked, "What method will we use to prove these triangles congruent?" voices rang out in unison, "Hypotenuse-Leg," even if there was no hypotenuse in the triangle. It was all about winning. These students didn't want to be caught losing this bet.

The end of the year arrived, and they all knew H-L well. Better yet, they all felt as though they won the bet.

Fast forward two years. To my great joy, a significant number of students in my geometry course returned for a year of Precalculus with me. The class even met in the same room. In the trigonometry section of Precalculus, we studied the Law of Sines. A subtopic in my Law of Sines lesson is the ambiguous case example, which illustrates the failure of A-S-S to form a unique triangle. There is only one exception, when the "A" represents a right angle, resulting in the H-L method of demonstrating uniqueness of a triangle.

During the moment considering the ambiguous case when H-L became relevant, I asked, "And how do we know this is a unique triangle?" I expected students to remember the redundancies: S-S-S, A-S-A, S-A-S, and A-A-S, and this year they did not disappoint.

"Side-Angle-Side," right on cue, the first person responded.

"No, Side-Side-Side," answered another, right on track.

A third chimed in, "Neither of those. Angle-Side-Angle."

The room is filled with screams of the words "side" and "angle," but not one "hypotenuse" or "leg."

They argued with each other for a bit. I was enjoying their passion and determination to outyell each other.

I turned out the lights, a technique they knew from elementary school that still worked.

Fourteen pairs of eyes quietly looked at me, begging to be told they were correct. I let the silence hang. The long silence made the next few minutes very, very sweet.

"I see I've finally won our bet."

The fourteen pairs of eyes looked at each other, confused, in a stunned silence. Then one person saw it and groaned. Eventually the whole room became loud with two words.

"Hypotenuse-Leg!" They were smiling in what they perceived to be victory, but I stood still, shaking my head slowly side to side. They were yelling, "Hypotenuse-Leg!"

"Too late."

Some students stood, pointing, insisting their victory, while others remained seated, laughing, and knowing it was over.

This was a fine moment, because now I was more certain they would never forget the H-L theorem when they completed the SAT the following year. I certainly didn't mind that no one paid up for losing our bet; I received something far more valuable.

Robert's Theorem

2013

Robert left class standing a little taller. His chest was slightly protruding away from his spine, and his shoulders leveled back slightly. He wore a self-satisfied smirk and strode from the room with long, purposeful movements. Class went well for him.

At the beginning of class, I asked students to draw a line segment and its perpendicular bisector. Students dutifully bent their heads over their papers and drew the illustration in their binders.

"Label the end points of the segment A and B. Label the intersection of the segment and the line as M."

They quietly added the labels to their illustrations.

"Choose any point on the perpendicular bisector and label it Z." I paused for added effect, "For 'zee' point."

"Ha, Ha, Ms. M.," said the snarky student in front. Others just shook their heads. By this point in the year, students laugh, not at my jokes but at me, for another predictably silly comment.

"Humor me by laughing," I said. "I write comments to your parents and for your college recommendations, remember," I added with a smirk.

Then the class erupted into laughter without mirth. It was my turn to shake my head and chuckle. I'd do anything to keep the students alert.

"Now see if you can find something interesting about 'zee' point. Go for it. Be creative. Let me suggest drawing some auxiliary lines."

I walked around the room holding my hands behind my back, watching the focused teens, and nodding as they revealed a myriad of extra lines, angles, and geometric shapes on their papers.

There was a photo of Jane Goodall on my wall, along with some other creative people who have changed our world: Cesar Chavez, Malala Yousafzai, Pablo Picasso, Virginia Woolf, Maya Angelou, Steve Jobs, and

Martin Luther King, for examples. Students asked early in the year about these images. I asked them to be patient. They will hear about them eventually. This day was Jane Goodall's day.

"I'm convinced," I said, "young people hold the key to solving our world's problems. You all, at your age, are so very creative, you'll likely find something maybe no one has ever seen or thought of before."

I thought they were ignoring me, or at least they were acting like it. But I continued.

"Take Jane Goodall, for example." They looked up. "She was chosen to accompany primate researchers to Africa before she had any degree. Why do you think she was chosen—even without experience?"

Kids shuffled. "So she could set up their tents, fetch their water, stuff like that?"

"Nah, she must have been someone's daughter."

"No," I said. "She was passionate. She was creative. Her youth and inexperience were strengths. These qualities allowed her to think of solutions to problems no one else previously considered. I think you, here and now, can come up with creative ideas perhaps no one has thought about before—even in geometric diagrams as simple as what you are considering today. So go for it. Find something interesting, form a conjecture, and let's see if we can prove it and make a theorem out of your ideas."

I continued my stroll around the room, nodding, and saying not-so-random things such as, "Interesting idea drawing that line," and "Ooh, I like your work here."

Robert became restless. He shifted around in his seat a lot, so I walked over to him. "I think I have something," he said.

I sent him to the board to draw his image and auxiliary lines. His illustration was simple. He added segments AZ and BZ to my drawing. "These segments have to have equal length."

"Really? Why?" I asked, trying to look very contemplative. Others in the room knitted their brows and chewed on their pencils.

"Triangles AZM and BZM must be congruent by Side-Angle-Side, so therefore AZ and BZ are also congruent because they are corresponding parts of congruent triangles."

I urged him on. "Do you think the result would be the same if you placed Z somewhere else on the perpendicular bisector?"

He identified a different "zee" point and demonstrated the result was the same.

"Wow," I said. "That's new." I looked around the room and asked if other people's work supported Robert's idea. They all nodded in agreement.

"Robert!" I was enthusiastic. "You found a new idea! Let's see if we can put words to it." With a little assistance, we eventually had, "Any point on the perpendicular bisector of a segment is equidistant to the endpoints of the segment."

"There are too many words in the theorem," came the general cry. We agreed to call it "Robert's Theorem," for short.

Robert's Theorem came up periodically in class even months later. We all looked at Robert and noted his brilliant addition to the geometry canon by nodding in his direction. Robert consistently beamed.

About fifteen years later, at a reunion event, Robert found me. "So, Ms. M., I was thirty years old before I realized my 'theorem' is in every geometry book published." I felt busted.

"Have you ever considered acting?" he asked.

Sleepy Time

2014

As I stood in front of my classroom, Stephen was sitting in a desk next to the wall on my left. He slid the desk so close to the wall that he could rest his head against it. His chair was twisted at an angle, and he seemed settled in for naptime. I noticed this before attendance. It's nine a.m., second period of the day.

"Stephen, buddy, you okay?" I asked. Stephen was a hard worker, on the wrestling team, and very involved in student government. Well loved by his peers, he was always game for gentle ribbing.

"Just tired, ma'am. Busy night."

"I'll do my best," I said, "to have an invigorating trig class to keep you alert and excited."

A couple other students snorted audibly. We all knew proving trig identities was not something on the top of the "exciting" list for the typical seventeen-year-old.

"Hey!" I said in response to the snorts, feigning offense. "Some of us are really excited by trig proofs!"

"I'll try my best, too, Ms. M."

Shortly thereafter, his head was back to resting against the wall, mouth opened, and he was deep in sleep. His neighbor poked at him. "Hey, Stephen," I heard him admonish.

Stephen jumped awake, his eyes bloodshot. "I'm here, I'm alert, What? Hypotenuse-Leg! Three-pi-over-two! No? Okay, then root-three-over-three?" His friends giggled and rolled their eyes.

We had three involved proofs on the board when we noticed Stephen was catching flies again. I put my index finger to my lips, turned out the lights, and we all tiptoed out of the room. I was fully expecting he would awaken when we walked out—it's impossible for more than a dozen people to leave the room of desks quietly and without bumps.

But he didn't awaken. He remained in the darkened room, leaning against the wall, mouth agape.

At a loss, I was in the hallway with thirteen teenagers to whom I'm supposed to teach trig proofs, not knowing where to go now. I started thinking Stephen's behavior was not normal. He was simply sleeping too deeply. I had my laptop in the hall and did a quick check on his medical records to see if he was diabetic or had another relevant health issue. I've learned from experience lethargy from diabetes is a red alarm.

Nope. Nothing was in his medical history. I fired up a quick alert to the nurse. I knew she would respond quickly and be here within a couple minutes.

I left the kids in the hallway and reentered the classroom alone. I was worried. I slid my hand over his temple and forehead. He was burning up. I guessed 104 degrees, which turned out to be accurate. But with my touch, he abruptly woke up.

Seeing no one else in the darkened room, he said, "Oh no! Did I miss wrestling?" *Oh*, I thought, *this will be such a good thing to remind him of when he returns to class.* But not now, he was too sick.

"I'm so sorry, Stephen. You're not going to wrestling today."

I called the nurse; she was already on her way.

He was absent for several days getting over his illness. I prepared for his return by supplying a fresh cover to a pillow I kept in a small bookshelf in the classroom.

He returned to class with big grins. "I'm so glad to be back! I was so sick!" He slipped into his old seat next to the wall. Others greeted him with pats on the shoulder.

I handed him the pillow and said, "This is for you." He was not sure how to respond but fell in sync with me by placing it on the wall and leaning his head against the pillow. I continued, "But please know it's important to stay home when you're sick."

"Yeah," continued his neighbor, "you could have passed on your bug to me."

"Stephen, you were worried about missing wrestling class. Were you not worried about missing math class?" He was not sure how to respond to my question.

"And when do you have wrestling?"

"3:30. After school." The class was chuckling now.

"What?" he said defensively, spreading his wings and looking around with his mouth opened wide.

The class took over the ribbing, "Dude, we have a nine a.m. math class. You fell asleep at about 9:15. You have Spanish, history, lunch, English and a science lab before wrestling."

"Yeah, but I can't miss wrestling. My coach would make me run. Not Ms. M. She would ask me if I was okay, take my temperature, and give me a pillow."

Math Class Is More than Math

2013-2016

I started the first class of the first day of my twenty-seventh year with energy. This class was quiet, unusual for eleventh grade. I amplified my efforts to engage these sleepy kids as the period progressed. Near the end of the fifty-minute period, one young man raised his hand.

"You're going to hate us," he deadpanned.

My tongue felt loose; I could feel cold air on the roof of my mouth. "And why would I hate you?" I quietly asked.

"Because we can't do math."

Gears spun swiftly in my head as I reevaluated my goals for the year. The service I needed to provide these young people was more difficult than polynomial division and the law of sines. They needed self-esteem, belief in themselves, and knowledge that I liked and valued them. It would be nice if they also had an appreciation for math. My self-set time frame? By the winter break in December.

October first, with a smirk on his face and after a good laugh over something-or-other, a student asked, "Are we your favorite class?"

"Yes," I said. I knew I had already reached my goal. I could tell, not by this question, but because these students were completing their homework diligently and were learning the math.

Teenagers are at an amazing time of life when their brains are expanding, their thoughts are surprising and refreshing, and their attitudes are challenging. I'm inexplicably drawn to the most vociferous students, the quirkiest students, and the most challenging students. Often, they are the ones to lead creative, interesting, and earth-shattering lives.

When I said, "Yes," I was in trouble. The following class period, students shuffled in, glancing at me, at each other, and at their books.

They were uncharacteristically quiet. I stood looking at them with my head tilted to the side.

"We thought we were your favorite class, Ms. M. We heard you told first period *they* were your favorite class."

Every now and again, there's someone who rubs me the wrong way. I'm human and have preferences like everyone else, but it's my job to serve everyone equally and well. I reflect upon a paraphrased quote credited to Abe Lincoln: "I don't like that man. I must get to know him better," and I choose to spend more time with these students.

Near the end of my thirty-four-year teaching career, Jonas appeared in my classroom, sitting to my right, about halfway towards the back of the room. I could see his peers' eyes rolling when he spoke, which was nearly all the time. I was not the only one challenged to enjoy spending time with Jonas. He responded to my requests to "come by my office for a chat." Once there, we talked math and sports. We compared families and traditions. We told jokes and fun stories. I began to enjoy Jonas, affirming Lincoln's idea. Comfortable with each other, I asked him to look out for a couple other students and help me get them to participate more—if Jonas could just talk just a little less... With a conspiratorial squint and thin smile, he said yes, he'd help me help others.

And with that, Jonas began listening to others, giving time and airspace and encouragement and positive comments to his peers, who stopped their eye-rolling.

At some point, the Jonas at the beginning of the year was forgotten and the sixteen members of the class became one body, one mass working together and talking themselves through challenging trig problems.

A week before graduation, two years after his first class with me, Jonas returned to visit. He had earned admission to the University of Pennsylvania but had chosen a different school he thought would fit him better.

"Everything changed for me that year in your class," he said. "I started getting friends and feeling better about myself and school."

State Tournament

2017

I was the oldest in the room. The meeting felt like a power play. The student was red-faced, looking down, and surrounded by adults in charge. People present included not only the student and me, but the Assistant Head of School, the department head, the dean, and the student's basketball coach.

The state championship playoff was the following week. The team was highly ranked and needed each player at his best.

The topic of the meeting: Jeff, a fifteen-year-old sophomore in my Geometry class. Jeff was failing math after earning a test grade nearly thirty percentage points below passing. The assembled adults, other than me, were in the process of removing Jeff from the team. They discussed Jeff's predicament as if he was not in the room. They were planning the next few months of his life for him. I wanted to serve Jeff better.

I focused on Jeff, orienting myself and my vision in his direction. His head was down. I realized his self-esteem was well rooted in his athletics. He knew the consequences of failing a course was removal from the team until a passing grade was earned.

I thought of my own children and how they felt about athletics. I remembered my ineffectiveness with Jack my first year in the classroom. I remembered the valuable lessons I learned as an athlete in high school and college. These lessons—teamwork, communication, working towards a common goal, working hard to achieve success while only sometimes achieving it, and the value of friendships—are sometimes more important than proving triangles congruent. Most importantly, I was acutely aware Jeff's identity was wound tightly around his basketball prowess.

By all conversation in the room, Jeff was to be removed from the team immediately.

Without letting my eyes move from Jeff, I spoke slowly. "Technically, Jeff, you are not currently failing the course. You have an incomplete."

He looked up, searchingly, knowing he can play with an incomplete.

The other adults in the room became silent. I was still looking at Jeff but was aware I was now the center of attention.

"I always give opportunities for make ups. You have not yet taken the opportunity. Jeff, would you like to take a make-up test?"

He looked at me, disbelieving.

"Part of the 'make up' process is to meet with me twice before you make another attempt at the test. I want to be sure you are ready to take the test again. I don't want to set you up to fail. Clearly, I'm the one who failed to teach you the material well enough, so I'll need to try again. Will you meet with me so I can do a better job?"

Jeff nodded vigorously.

"And Jeff, I see you have some serious obligations to your team on the basketball court this week, so let's schedule our meeting times for next week."

The head of the division spoke, "But the quarter grades are due on Friday."

"I'm sure we can offer an incomplete grade for this quarter. I'm betting we can have a complete grade for him only a week after the due date."

The train was derailed, but a new train left the station.

It was Tuesday. On Wednesday, Thursday, and Friday, Jeff was on the basketball court as a starting player.

Seven a.m. on Monday, he arrived in my office, wide awake. "Let's start, Ms. M."

And with that, we focused and moved forward.

Sounds

2018

I heard it loud and clear—flatulence. Class was in session. We were discussing something I thought was important which I can't now remember. I nonchalantly walked towards the windows, opened them, then walked towards the door, opening it, not missing a beat.

Because of my hearing loss from the tumor, I could no longer tell the direction of sounds, so I could not discern the source. No matter, class would go on.

Then it happened again. I could hear some students begin to twitter, but I had no reaction and continued to conduct class without missing a beat.

Then it happened *again*. Students were laughing louder now, clutching their sides and slipping off their chairs. *Every now and again*, I thought, *there is an immature class*. These folks were sixteen to seventeen years old. I stayed stoic, modeling maturity. I was a little disgusted with them. I tried not to roll my eyes.

Then the flatulence happened again, and students were completely unable to control themselves. Only one student sat still, face red and holding a stern and worried expression.

"Justin, would you like to use the restroom? Or maybe see the nurse?" I asked, wishing to save the young man from his embarrassment and becoming increasingly impatient with the others in the room.

As he rose, the fifth loud and juicy flatulence sound filled the room, and students could barely stay in their seats.

Red-faced Justin slinked towards the front of the room, pulled his cell phone from his pocket, and handed it to me as the sixth sound emerged from the small box.

"I'm fine, Ms. M., it's just my ringtone."

And the class howled, not at Justin, but at my reaction.

Navigating Moguls

Fall 2019

Educating children and teens during a global pandemic held challenges. Our school experimented with different schedules, trying to find a sweet spot of serving students well and staying safe. Our school opted for longer class periods and fewer meeting times while online. We were going to experiment with two-hour math classes for a trimester. During Parents' Night, some parents asked how I could possibly get through a year's worth of material in fifty-five days. The thought was that surely a typical fifteen-year-old could not have sufficient time to let the material "sink in." The parents also were a little emotional. "However, will my fifteen-year-old stay focused on math for the whole two-hour class?"

"Those concerns have certainly been on my mind," I replied. As a veteran teacher, I had some tricks up my sleeve for navigating bumps I had never seen before. Throughout the semester, I tried new things, constantly adjusting strategies to fit the novel challenges. We settled quickly into a productive routine that included strategies for spiraling, repetition, fresh starts, fun surprises, and regular check-ins—components of my previous class periods but with greater intention, intensity, and diligence. I searched for links between ideas in math that would make our studies seem connected and would deepen students' understanding. A side benefit, I hoped, would be added fascination with mathematics. Pascal's Triangle was one of those ideas.

It was my eighth-to-last day in the classroom. I was feeling nostalgic about ending my teaching career and was demonstrating the skills and knowledge I had amassed over the previous three-plus decades of classroom service. Between class periods of an algebra class, I sat and recorded for those questioning parents the following description of a successful day in the classroom.

As students filter into the room, I encourage the early arrivals to begin writing Pascal's Triangle for review on the whiteboard. Humoring me by doing what they perceive as busy work, they begin.

1
1 1
1 2 1
1 3 3 1
1 4 6 4 1....

Each number in a row is formed by adding two subsequent values in the previous row. These specific values have begun to be very familiar to them; jumping out at them when the pattern appears in other places.

Beside the student-created triangle of values, I have written a fashionable "8" on the classroom whiteboard, denoting the number of days remaining in school this year. I point out 8 is a Fibonacci number. "What's that?" the curious minds reply. We record and explore the Fibonacci Sequence. I observe the "so what" images on the faces of my charges. Pulling up our old friend, Pascal's Triangle, I show them where the Fibonacci Sequence occurs in the triangle. Last week's Pascal's Triangle adventure included the display of the powers of 2 (found by adding the values of each row) and powers of 11 (example: 11^3 = 1331, the numbers in the row beginning 1-3). The previous blog assignment had students find something novel (to them) about the triangle, and today we see the Fibonacci Sequence in the famed pattern of numbers. I remind them what I said when they first learned about this triangular pattern, "When you least expect to see Pascal's Triangle, expect it." My audience appears non-plussed.

Now we move on to the next idea: counting possibilities in flips of a penny. Barely five minutes later, I'm met with groans as our old friend, Pascal's Triangle, reveals herself in the display of heads and tails. (For example, in four flips of a coin, there is 1 way for the result to be all heads, 4 ways for the result to be three heads and one tail, 6 ways for the result to be two heads and two tails, and so forth, following the pattern of the row in Pascal's Triangle that begins 1 – 4 – 6 …) I remind them again, "When you least expect it, expect it."

With Pascal's Triangle neatly tucked away, students purchase the notion it's time to move on. Our next idea is a standard Algebra II concept: sum and differences of cubes. The nine-minute movie in which I am the movie star moves swiftly for students. Their comments convey the "Pulling-the-Rabbit-From-The-Hat" proof was "satisfying," and they're "so happy to be back doing algebra." We review the concept, working together on some harder factoring problems featuring the sum and difference of cubes. Then they move on to binomial expansion.

Binomial Expansion is a topic usually reserved for PreCalculus. Students have another nine-minute video to watch, with basic information featuring their favorite movie star (that would be me). When 1-3-3-1 appears in the expansion of $(a+b)^3$, some students groan. I walk around the room, unable to hide my smirk. Some don't see our Old Friend until distributing $(a+b)^4$ and seeing the coefficients 1-4-6-4-1, and others need to see 1-5-10-10-5-1 before they believe Pascal's Triangle lies before them in all her glory. I hear several words and phrases—"No!" and "You're kidding." Some students are speechless while others wax on about how absolutely crazy it is this singular pattern has now been applied in multiple seemingly disparate ways. These exclamations of surprise are the climax to the two-hour class and occur in the final fifteen of the 120 minutes. The next task, which occurs in next year's math course, is how these seemingly disparate ideas all appear in the same simple display.

What made this class successful? What helped students focus? Different ideas. Increasingly challenging notions. A variety of presentations of material. And of course, a thread—such as Pascal's Triangle—pulling it all together. Humor also helps, even though many students had never experienced math humor before. A "math joke" is an oxymoron to many people in our culture, but not to my students. Review, repetition in small bites. Surprises. Memorable moments. Multiple connections. Deeper meanings. I don't think any of the students will ever forget Pascal's Triangle. And, of course, developing classes such as this kept me well entertained intellectually and gave me energy to develop more lessons with similar positive results.

Is It Dinner Time?

Spring 2020

My phone rang. It was seven p.m. Because we were in a global pandemic, classes were taught online. I wanted to support students and parents, and to minimize the trouble caused by this serious disruption, I had distributed my personal cell phone number. "Call anytime before eight p.m. and after eight a.m.," I had said.

Without introduction, he began in full-throated bellow. "I can't believe the assignment you gave my daughter! She spent two hours, working hard, trying to get this material. She wouldn't even come down for dinner."

This parent was angry. I had given too large and challenging an assignment, and he was beside himself. I must be a terrible teacher.

"Good evening," I measured. "I'm Ms. Mariner. To whom am I speaking?"

I don't think he wanted to identify himself after his initial outburst, but I insisted. We needed to work together. Chastised, he introduced himself, identifying his daughter by name. Then he launched into another tirade but with about half the volume. The themes—too much work, too demanding.

I explained that students were given a limit to the length of time they were to work on their math assignment. If they chose to work longer, then it was their choice, not a class requirement. I reiterated this nearly every day, so his daughter couldn't claim ignorance to this policy.

"Wait a minute," I said. "Is she still working on the assignment?"

"Yes!" he yelled.

"Like, right now?"

"*Yes!*" he screamed even louder. "I've never seen her stressed like this before."

"And is she entertained? I mean, is she focused and interested or is she pulling out her hair?"

"She's so focused, she won't come down for dinner or talk with us."

"Focused on math? Are you sure?" I asked.

"Yes, she tried to show me her calculations and illustrations, but I didn't understand. I just know she's working too hard. She was talking about trigonometry applications and our roof and driveway. We just want to have dinner. This is not like our daughter."

I thought of Archimedes, who was so focused on a math problem he had no idea his town was being ravaged by sword-wielding Romans.

This is going to be easy, I thought. The father clearly didn't understand what was happening. "I'm so impressed with her perseverance! She has qualities an employer will really appreciate!"

Silence from the parent.

"She's amazing," I continued. "She's developing wonderful problem-solving skills…and she's demonstrating exceptional focus. Looks like she's enjoying the math. Would you say that? Would you agree? Fast forward ten years, these wonderful qualities will still be there, and she'll be so valued by her employer."

The father was silent.

What made this exchange additionally surprising was we were in the middle of a global pandemic when classes were held online. I was teaching two-hour math classes on zoom. We met every other day. Most parents were complaining their kids were not getting enough math. Here, I had a parent complaining his daughter had too much.

"Are you there?" I asked. He was.

I asked him to put her on the phone.

"Ms. Mariner!" she said breathlessly. Speaking quickly, she continued, "Did you know the inverse tangent of the grade of the road is the angle of elevation and is the same concept as the pitch of a roof and the slope of a line?"

"Amanda," I interrupted, "that is so exciting! You are so clever! I'm so impressed with your efforts, discovery, and focus!" Before she could say more, "Now go have dinner with your family. They miss you at the dinner table."

"Is it dinner time?" Amanda asked quietly.

The Gifts

Through the Years

"I wouldn't *go* there," Brian whispered in my ear. "My dad is serious about his ice cream."

Brian's dad and I were discussing what ice cream was best. Brian was correct; his dad was passionate.

"If you've never had Margo's Ice Cream, then how do you know?" He was animated and loud.

"But Ben and Jerry's!" I love the creative flavors, the high caloric and fat content of their product, and the fact Jerry attended my Alma Mater.

He countered with a description of the expansive menu at Margo's Ice Cream Shop, the unforgettable nature of Margo's creamy dessert due to real, organic, full-o-fat cream, cane sugar, and natural sweeteners, and what he presumed to be my own inexperience with ice cream. I knew when the bear was against the wall and would keep fighting, so I shook my head and admitted defeat, simply wanting to remove myself from this silly passionate argument.

He harumphed, knowing he had not really changed my mind but had bullied me into agreeing.

Parent's Weekend in the eighties and early nineties was like that—silly discussions, passionate parents about random unconnected things, embarrassed teens, and a general feeling of camaraderie common between teachers and parents. My exchange with Brian's dad was one of many and would have been forgettable, except...

Several weeks later, a brown, unlabeled box arrived through the post addressed to me. It was forty-inch by forty-inch by forty-inch. I could barely reach my arms around it enough to carry it. I needed a sharp knife to remove the tape and noticed this was no ordinary cardboard—it was a full three-quarters inch thick. Pulling up the flaps, I saw white Styrofoam in what appeared to be a solid block completely filling the box. As I birthed the Styrofoam cube from the box, I saw it was split around the middle and was also well taped. I cut the tape, opened the egg, revealing a six-inch cube inside an otherwise solid white albumen of Styrofoam. The outside layer of the center cube-yolk was well-sealed dry ice. As I pulled the packaged dry ice away carefully, a single small container of ice cream, still frozen solid, remained in the center. From Margo's. Shipped to Colorado from Ohio.

Excited and chuckling, I rushed home, wondering how to appropriately dispose of all the packaging, and enjoyed a single spoonful of the mint chocolate chip ice cream.

I conceded defeat in a phone call. The ice cream was smooth and rich. The fat content was high. I could feel the cream stick to the roof of my mouth. I placed the small container, minus one bite, in my freezer. I planned to savor the special ice cream for a long time.

Several days later, some of my dorm charges were hanging out watching a movie in my apartment. I left to take "check" to be sure everyone was "in" for the night. When I returned, the empty ice cream container was in the trash.

"Totally awesome ice cream," said one of them, still licking the spoon.

One of my kind colleagues worked with student Alex every day. He struggled, but Ms. Alveolar took pleasure seeing a student willing to come to school a little early each day for an extra bump in understanding and grades. During the year, he grew and learned enough to open doors in any career option, but most importantly, he succeeded in the fine art of persistence. They clearly developed a special friendship because of the sweat, the regularity, and a common determination to have Alex earn a grade a little more commensurate with his efforts.

When his mom said she had a small present for Ms. Alveolar to recognize the special efforts she made with Alex, no one was surprised. None of us ever teach for the presents people bring, but a teacher's heart is warmed when a parent or student recognizes extra efforts. Alex's mom delivered the present quietly in a cardboard box, labeled with professional address labels for her dentistry business. She left the box in the center of Ms. Alveolar's desk. Accompanying the box was a card, "For Ms. Alveolar, Thank you for your work with Alex."

Ms. Alveolar was certain the box with the professional address must have been repurposed, until she opened it to find one hundred individually wrapped, neon pink toothbrushes bearing Alex's mom's full name, followed by a comma and DDS. Ms. Alveolar generously shared her bounty with teachers on the same hallway. She had enough to keep sharing her bounty for two years.

The gift seemed to keep giving. About a dozen years after Alex graduated, Ms. Alveolar was handed a tardy pass for a student late to class, signed by the dentist. Accompanying the pass was a handful of individually wrapped, neon pink toothbrushes, handed to her with a look of confusion by the student with newly cleaned teeth.

Jody was a beloved advisee and student who lived in my dorm—a young woman who became pregnant her tenth-grade year. By the time she arrived at my door, she had been in denial for five months and was showing. She decided to return home to her family and face her next steps with their support.

On the way to the airport, I took her to an ice cream parlor for sundaes. She lifted the maraschino cherry by the stem and wiggled it in the air.

"You know, I had sex exactly *once*. And now—" she looked at the cherry and smirked. "What I'd give to take this back right now," she looked from the cherry to me. We shared a moment of sadness that morphed into laughter, letting our teacher-student relationship melt into a combination of mother-daughter and friends.

Later that year, a small package arrived in the mail. It held a small, wooden, hand-decorated, heart-shaped box. On the back was a personalized message in black sharpie, followed by, "Love, Jody." She had taken care with the design, cutting red and black ribbons to cover the box in a pattern. She may have spent twenty minutes or so decorating the box but also planned, purchased the materials, and crafted this project from her heart. It stayed on my dresser holding a few pieces of jewelry for years.

Part 5:
The Career that Keeps on Giving

"Learn to light a candle in the darkest moments of someone's life. Be the light that helps other see; it is what gives life its deepest significance."

– Roy T. Bennett, The Light in the Heart[1]

As my students left my classroom at the end of each year, I'd look after them, longing for further touch. My eyes, my soul, and sometimes my hand would extend towards them, wanting to know where they'd go and what they'd find on their life journeys. When I'd send them on their way, I'd get a little choked up. Some students would linger, not quite wanting to leave. In those awkward few minutes, I'd say:

"When you ride your bike by my home, stop in to say hello.

I'll always remember you. Come back and say hello.

Even if I can't remember you, I know I will love seeing you in twenty or thirty years. Please find me and say hello."

During reunions or at random times in my life, a former student would reach out and describe places traveled, sights seen, jobs held, and goals attained. The salespeople at the local Chevy dealership marveled at their

---

1) Bennett, Roy T. *The Light in the Heart: Inspirational Thoughts for Living Your Best Life.* 2nd ed. Roy Bennett, 2021, 20.

boss and I remembering each other. "What? You were her high school math teacher?" Reunions are particularly joyful—to see new families and chosen careers.

Babies

2013

I'm not sure why I answered the phone—it was an unknown number from Texas. But I did; I was rewarded by a voice familiar in another life.

Dana, dispassionate about math but passionate about making the world simply more fun, began the conversation with a contagious energy, bringing me back the twenty years since I had seen her last. She was doing well, working in the treasury department in Washington, DC. She was well-connected with her classmates from twenty years ago and enjoying the company of many friends. Still mourning the loss of her beloved brother, she had developed an even deeper bond with her parents back home in Austin.

Then there was a pregnant pause. She had called for a reason.

"Jean, I want to be a mom. I don't have any partner prospects. I'm now thirty-six. Should I get artificially inseminated and have a baby?"

Now the pause was very pregnant. "Um, Dana? I'm your high school math teacher. Have you tried talking with your mom? A close friend?"

"They are biased. You always looked out for my best interest, and you told me I could always contact you, so here I am. I'm asking you, should I go ahead and try to have a baby on my own?"

"Dana?" I was at a sincere loss. "This is a big decision for you. I haven't seen you in almost twenty years."

"Does it matter?" she asked.

I asked her about the specifics of her interest in having children. She'd always dreamed of being a mom. Her clock was ticking. She was done waiting. She was financially stable and could do this on her own.

I was more comfortable avoiding the topic and thus utilized a strategy that worked for me in the past—assume she needed verification for a decision she had already made.

"Dana, you've made a major effort to find me. You overcame obstacles to find my phone number and call me. I think you already know what you want. I'm so happy to support you in your decision."

Eight weeks later, Dana called again—pregnant.

I sent off a baby quilt and letters of congratulations for the birth of her daughter not quite a year later.

A year passed. My phone rang. I could see it was Dana on the other end.

"I want another," she says. "I became pregnant so fast the first time that I have enough sperm remaining from the donor, so if I do this again, my children could be full siblings. Should I do it?"

This was easier than the first time. "Dana, calling me like this indicates to me that you really want another child. I don't think you'll ever regret having a second child." We had a short chat before she rushed off the phone to make the appointments.

Eight weeks later, Dana called once more—pregnant again.

Teacher attention can be a powerful missive with a lifetime of impact. Teenagers are fragile, vulnerable, impressionable, and passionate. If the missive sent to a fertile mind is one of support and care, the bounty is a gift returned tenfold. I shake my head in disbelief; something right must have happened with my missive to Dana.

Swimming an Alcatraz Escape

2017

I arrived at the airport in San Jose in the fall to be met by Emily and Fern. Thirty years earlier, Emily and Fern were my charges in the math classroom, the pool, and in the dorm. I hadn't seen them since they were eighteen and I was twenty-seven. Them now forty-six and me at fifty-five, I understood a lot can happen in thirty years. My breathing was shallow and rapid. I calmed myself using the mantra: *Emily and Fern are strong, caring, and wonderful women. Emily and Fern are strong, caring, and wonderful women.* Indeed, Emily was a CEO of her own company and Fern served on the board of the independent boarding school she attended. They raised strong, productive, and beautiful children.

My steps through the airport were strangely deliberate and surreal. I bit my lip when I placed my bag on the escalator heading down to the baggage claim area. Then suddenly—you never heard such hooting, hollering, and general carrying-on as we clung to each other, simply amazed by what we were endeavoring to do with, and for, each other.

Emily and Fern were fifteen-year-old high school students when I had the brain surgery to remove a large tumor. As terrified teenagers, they avoided me and did not know how to simply "be" around me. They were part of the record-breaking relay team, and they were at the Weddington-Schlafly debate. I took Fern to the hospital after she'd eaten a plant on a bizarre whim one Friday night. We had years of trials and tribulations together. I was the target of their teenage antics and the recipient of teasing after my dates.

Upon hearing of a recurrence of my tumor nearly thirty years later, Emily called. "We'd like to swim an 'Escape from Alcatraz' in your honor. We know you love open water swimming, and you always encouraged us to go outside our comfort zone. This seems to be a perfect way to honor you."

I was speechless.

"And," she said, "Our families, some friends, and some other swim team members will be joining us on the swim." My heart skipped a beat. We'd be a team of about a dozen.

"Um," she continued, "Fern and I have always been embarrassed at our fifteen-year-old selves for not supporting you. We'd like to be better this time."

The swim turned out even more special. I was able to join them on the swim.

That night, after greeting each other at the airport, we caught up over clam chowder and white wine as we discussed children, jobs, projects, partners, and more. Always the consummate math teacher, I discussed planning for the swim.

"We will swim about an hour before high tide. Think about the value of the first derivative," I began. They humored me with the discussion. "With the current flowing westward at 1.5 mph, if we swim 2 mph, let's set up a vector analysis." On our third glass of wine, the conversation shifted to memories of their awakening at the Weddington-Schlafly debate and their awkward youth on the swim team.

"That night at the debate changed my life," said Fern. "My eyes were opened to how so many people viewed women."

Emily concurred, "Back then, I had never seen anyone with opinions so different from mine. I also learned we *must* stand up for our rights."

"I had no idea that night would change so many of us," I added. It was the best five-hundred-dollar risk I'd ever taken.

Emily mused, "You know, I don't shave my legs anymore."

"Neither do I," added Fern. As our thoughts moved to small hairs taped on a card, we dissolved into giggles.

A day later, dressed in our wetsuits, caps, goggles, and timing straps, we walked toward the pier docking the ferry that would take us to the island, so we could properly escape. We met our teammates and boarded the ferry together, joining the several hundred other swimmers participating in the escape. Seals were sunbathing on the shore. I reassured Fern that there must not be any sharks around because the seals were comfortably resting. As the ferry made progress into the bay, I checked my pulse:

150 and climbing. The first battle would be to relax. On a ferry packed with anxious and excited swimmers, relaxing was no small feat. Thankfully, the trip to Alcatraz was short, and we adjusted our goggles as the start of the swim was announced.

Shuffling towards the side of the boat, the three of us with our arms wrapped around each other watched others make the jump into the churning, green waters of the San Francisco Bay. Emily was beaming, soaking in the moment with all its excitement and joy. This was all-in-a-day's experience for her; her well-worn wetsuit revealed her experience in open water.

Fern looked nervous. "There are no seals," she observed meaningfully.

I wanted to point out, "If there are no seals, then there are sharks," is not the logical equivalent of "If there are seals, then there are no sharks." Indeed, that's the inverse error, as I had taught her in 1987, but there was no time for a math lesson, though I was happy for the mental diversion. For the next moment, our bodies were suspended in midair over the deep, cold, and turbulent bay. The trip from the platform of the boat to the surface of the water seemed to be in slow motion so we could experience each nanosecond in full.

A plunge is different from the start of other open water races. In addition, each plunge in this race is different from any other. The boat is loud, frantic, crowded, dry, and warm with the hundreds of people attempting the swim, while in the water, it's cold, silent, solitary, and a striking emerald green. I wiggled free of my clinging swimming partners and of others making their own adjustments and began to let my arms pull me through the water towards the shore.

As the swimmers spread out on their own personal and independent silent journeys, I drank in the image of the red bridge over my right shoulder. Rolling over on my back to take in the full 360-degree view for which this area is famous, I gauged my progress towards The-Land-of-Chocolate-Plenty by looking in the rearview mirror, that is, by watching the white rocks and buildings on Alcatraz move into the more distant past as I progressed towards Ghirardelli Square. I drew my chin into my chest and laughed out loud at the insanity of this task. Then I took one last look at Alcatraz and focused on the shimmering city that was our destination.

Threading the needle into the relatively small entrance of San Francisco's Aquapark, the silence of the swim was broken by horns, cheers, and claps of those great California residents cheering us on from the piers.

Then my hands hit bottom; my feet touched the smooth piles of rocks; I sloshed through the shallow water, gathering my land legs; I ran through the finish arch. A smiling woman placed bling around my neck, and I pushed my way through the crowd of spectators and swimmers who swam faster than me to find my team. As the dozen people Emily and Fern had recruited to swim with us trickled in to the finish, our group grew by one person at a time. We greeted each other with joy and enthusiasm, but we looked to the water, straining to identify others in our clan just arriving. Ambulances flashing their lights reminded us that some don't reach the shore on their own accord. We glanced nervously to see if any of the people traveling that route were wearing Fern's distinctive wetsuit. Emily pointed to the far end of Aquapark, where the cigarette buoy marks the entrance to the swimming area, and correctly identified Fern's distinctive bob in the water. My heart returned to the center of my chest.

We reached out to her, instinctively, as she touched bottom, smiling. "I did it."

Indeed, what we did together was to add another layer to our already deep relationship and to solidify the joy of the lifelong learning adventure beginning thirty years earlier.

Jicama and Headlights

2020

"You had such an impact on me," Cal said at his thirtieth high school reunion. "I think of you every day. And Kira feels the same way." Kira and Cal developed a fine friendship in high school and have stayed in touch over the years.

Humbled, I glanced down, "Well, now," I started, "that can't be true. I was only your high school psychology teacher over thirty years ago."

We revisited the moments which changed his life.

"You invited Kira and me for dinner in your apartment," Cal reminded me.

I nodded, remembering that I often had small groups of students for dinner. We'd prepare food together, set the table, and sit with linens and candlesticks to share time and a meal.

"Right when Kira and I arrived, you ushered us into the kitchen and gestured towards the cutting boards, knives, and stuff for the salad—likely lettuce, celery, carrots, tomatoes, green peppers, jicama, and sunflower seeds. Kira and I recognized everything except what I now know is jicama. I leaned in towards her and whispered, asking what that brown, ugly rock-like thing was. You moved in to help—peeled it, cut a few strips, and invited us to try it."

As he spoke, I remembered how amazed I was that they had reached fifteen years of life without having eaten a jicama fruit.

"Then there was that moment," Cal continued, "that crunch that changed my life. It was truly love at first chomp. I remember looking at Kira and her eyes were wide open with surprise.

"So," Cal continued, "jicama is likely my favorite food. I have jicama every day on my salad, and I think of you each time I prepare it."

If my legacy is to introduce foods that bring joy to people, then I'm thinking that's alright.

"But there's more," he continued. "Do you remember driving us to the mall for shopping on Saturdays?"

"Of course." My mind flashed to the time when I drove the forty-four-passenger yellow school bus northward to the large mall.

"You always parked far from the entrance because of the size of the bus. We'd walk through the parking lot to the mall entrance together," Cal began, looking searchingly at me, wondering if I remembered. I did not.

"One afternoon," he continued, "we noticed a car with its headlights on. You reached in the open window and turned off the headlights."

"That sounds like me," I said, remembering the days when car headlights didn't automatically turn off and car windows could be left open without fear. Leaving the headlights on might result in a fully drained car battery.

Cal nodded with a smirk. "I remember asking you why you did that, and you said, 'To be kind.' You didn't want anyone to return to a car with a dead battery.

"So," Cal smiled broadly, "I always look to see if I can be helpful to someone in some small way. Practicing random acts of kindness, especially when I will never be recognized for my good deed, has me feeling pretty good about myself and the world. I always look to see if I could turn off someone's headlights, or if there's something I could do to make someone's life a little easier. That's the kind of world I want to live in."

If my legacy is to spread this type of kindness, I feel satisfied.

Never did I think things as mundane as the meals I shared or the rides I provided to students would include lessons remembered for a lifetime.

Forward and Focused

2012

So, there he was, standing in front of me with his well-coiffed wife and well-scrubbed pair of children: one boy, one girl. All were smiling at the high school twenty-year reunion as they chatted with me, Mark's former math teacher, former chaperone on a ski trip, and former comrade in an ambulance to the ER to stabilize a broken arm after a backward, blind, and boozed morning run on a black diamond.

The chitchat was lovely all around, but could have gone astray when his wife said, "Please, tell us some stories about Mark in high school."

I glanced at Mark, then did a double take. He stepped back, letting his eyeballs protrude from their sockets, and shaking his head with a spasmodic "no." I noted that my mouth was frozen in a vertical "O" shape, which I changed immediately into a smile with my head cocked to one side.

I'm good with platitudes and veiled references. His wife giggled when I said, "Times in the library were so fun—it was like a party." The reality: Mark had stolen a faculty member's keys, somehow acquired a keg, and was host to a keg party in the library one Saturday night into Sunday morning. Mark appeared relieved when I made it clear I would not reveal anything unsavory about his teenage years.

I continued, "And we skied together. Once. Mark is a great skier; I couldn't keep up on the black diamonds." Mark shot me a hard look; his wife beamed at Mark; he looked down at his children.

"Really, Dad? But you always go on the greens with me," said the youngest.

"It's more fun for me that way," Mark replied.

He looked at me with a grin. "You were such a good bus driver. You were particularly unflappable on our early morning ski trips."

We all have moments in our past that embarrass us. As youth, we are allowed to try new things. Indeed, we need to be adventurous so we can learn our limits. We also will inevitably grow up, change, and become better people. Indeed, let's hope we do; no one should be stuck as a fifteen-year-old—or even a twenty-three-year-old—forever. Silently, to myself in front of Mark and his family, I'm repeating the mantra, *People are allowed to grow up*.

"So, Mark," I began. "What do you do now?" He certainly looked like he was traveling through life facing forward with his eyes opened.

He cleared his throat briefly and looked down, so I was sure he was thinking of his many risk-taking, learning moments during his time as a teenager. "I'm a high school administrator in charge of discipline at our independent school."

Mrs. Wilmacar

2021

In the first months of my retirement, I cleaned out files, books, papers, unfinished lessons, interesting articles, and toys for learning geometry. Amongst the thirty-plus-year collection of teaching supplies was a collection of books from over sixty years ago, yellowed with age and labeled in the clean angled script of someone who had enjoyed penmanship class in the 1930s: *Mrs. Iris Wilmacar.*

Upon her retirement in 1987, she passed along a set of her books, her favorite lessons, and information about activities such as building polyhedra—an activity my classes completed with great relish. She had correctly anticipated I would use and enjoy her materials.

Mrs. Wilmacar taught me Algebra II in 1976. Nearing the end of her career, she sat at the overhead projector and used transparencies to teach conic sections and a proof of the quadratic formula. She handwrote tests, mimeographed them, and clucked softly when we collected our test papers and immediately held them to our noses to smell the sweet scent of the copy dye. She lived and breathed teaching. Years later, I understood that everything she saw in the grocery, on her drives home, during summer vacations, and in her family life became inspiration for developing lessons for the classroom. I learned she would always be a teacher—up to and including her last year of life. Like the great Jimi Hendrix, she slept with her instrument.

I maintained a friendship with Mrs. Wilmacar. She attended celebrations for my wedding, and I attended her husband's memorial. We chatted in her living room, overlooking a Connecticut woodland. When she lived in a retirement apartment, I visited her and her dog. My visits became about once a year because I lived out of state. In my last visits, she was in memory care, having lost most of her memories.

"It's all empty in there," she said, pointing to her temple.

I thought, *She's a shell of who she once was.*

In our last visit, she gave me the lesson I hold dearest—how to age gracefully.

I arrived at the door with flowers, a grin, and a hymnal from her church. She liked to sing right up until the end. She could sing all four verses of "Oh Beautiful," not missing one word even through her profound dementia. Her feet were elevated and greatly swollen. The room held a single bed, a bedstand table, a reclining chair on which she was sitting, and posterboards with large pictures of people—her mother, daughters, sister, and husband. One of the staff members brought me a folding chair.

Mrs. Wilmacar looked at me searchingly as I sat. When she realized I was a visitor and not a health care provider, she said, "Well now, I have no idea who you are, but you are visiting me, so you must be a friend. Come tell me about who you are and all you have done since you saw me last."

I obliged, and she beckoned me to tell her more. Indeed, I repeated the same story a handful of times; it was fresh to her each time. She smiled and nodded and asked questions, attentive to each word.

A nurse on the floor walked me to the locked exit, accompanied by Mrs. Wilmacar and her walker. I felt the need to let the nurse know about this wonderful woman.

"She was my math teacher," I started, "but she was more. She was the first to bring you a meal if you were sick. She was always there with an ear and a kind word. She took my mother out for walks when my mother was sad. She carefully attended to new students at the school."

Mrs. Wilmacar looked at me quizzically, not even recognizing herself.

The nurse turned to Mrs. Wilmacar and said, "What a great mentor you are." It was particularly meaningful that the nurse used the present tense.

Now, about twenty years since Mrs. Wilmacar passed, I tell my students to please keep swinging by to say hello, even if I have lost my memory. I've rehearsed Mrs. Wilmacar's words: "I have no idea who you are, but you are visiting me, so you must be a friend. Come tell me about who you are and all you have done since you have seen me last."

Epilogue: Letters

2023

In preparation for publication, I contacted many of the students featured in my stories. The following are a selection of responses. When I read them, I think some of these folks, now nearing retirement, must be wearing rose-colored glasses.

Jack, of desk-throwing fame, responded nearly immediately. He was also the young man who helped me when I was in trouble on the streets of Leningrad. He wrote:

> Dear Ms. Miller-Mariner,
>
> What a real joy it is to hear from you after such a passage of time. Your patience and guidance made a significant and positive impact on me…and trust me, I know what a handful I was back then! I owe you thanks.
>
> For my side, as you may recall, I attended your old rival college, and from there went straight into the corporate world. In my mid-forties, I experienced a major conversion of heart, thus began practicing and living my Catholic faith. Two years later, I dropped everything and entered seminary. Currently, I am in my sixth year of seminary priestly formation. God willing, I'll be ordained into the transitional Diaconate and from there into the priesthood.
>
> In the meantime, know you are in my prayers, and I'm looking forward to reading your piece.
>
> With best regards and In Christ,
> Jack

Cal, of Jicama and Headlights, also answered quickly with enthusiasm:

> I love this! And honestly, it's what I needed right now—to know that I have a positive impact on people and make a difference.
>
> In the interest of full disclosure, my addled brain recalls making jicama sticks and marinating them in like juice and sugar.

Emily, swimmer in high school and in the Escape from Alcatraz, and present at the Weddington-Schlafly debate writes:

> I had a good chuckle reading this, Jean! I tell this story (about the high school swim record being broken) to anyone who will listen. I did eventually get the olive branch added to the dove in college and then Lissa had hers removed—no fair.
>
> The piece about the Weddington-Schlafly debate is especially timely. I'm learning there are lots of parallels in sustainability and women's rights. Might be a good research project.
>
> You were such a force for us in high school! I can't believe you spent a whole paycheck on that event. I wouldn't be the person I am now without you as a teacher and coach at such an impressionable age.

Lissa, swimmer and participant in the group tattoo-fest, writes:

> Hello Jean!
>
> Your essays are awesome—those stories brought me back to my sixteen-year-old self! So fun! I love it.
>
> I hope to see you on an upcoming adventure of some sort. But I'll have to just be a cheerleader if it includes a frigid bay swim.
>
> I had tattoos of a dove, olive branch, and swirling earth behind it ALL removed. Unfortunately, I'm not a very quick study and got inked up again.

Cathy, MVP Swimmer for two years and anchor for the record-breaking 400 yard freestyle relay, now an aquatics educator:

> Yes! I vividly remember opening that card and exclaiming out loud for all to hear! Those hairs taped inside have been etched into my memory forever! Our thoughts also went to…are these from her legs? Armpits? We did not want to have to explain our reaction to those around us. This was an epic move by you for sure! Well done!
>
> I loved reading this from your perspective—especially now as I am a swim coach! How I loved swimming and am so very appreciative of all your work, time, and energy to make it happen. I remember my first year it was possible that we'd not have a swim team. My roommate made me go to volleyball. You entered the gym at the end of practice and said, "See you at the pool tomorrow." I was thrilled to have enough of us to make a team.

Natalie, 500 yard swimmer and activist at the Weddington-Schlafly debate, stayed in contact with me for many years. Her response to the stories:

> About Swimming and GAFFO:
>
> Jean, I loved reading this! I remember being terrified of competing, and I remember false starting in a race. I do remember that you were always on our side, and that was important to me, especially at that time of my life. We were lucky to have you.
>
> I'm glad you wrote about GAFFO. How GAFFO ideology dominated the school culture and how all boys (and men!) treated me left me feeling so terrible. I think GAFFO was reflecting the culture we were living in, and it's important that people know what we went through.
>
> Having parents love you unconditionally is one thing. Having a teacher love you unconditionally is one of the best gifts. Thank you for that. I know I wasn't easy to love back then.
>
> About the Weddington-Schlafly debate: Jean, this brought me to tears!!!! I had forgotten so many of the details, and you reminded me of many.

The debate was just one way you stood up for women. You showed us what it's like to be a strong and loving woman, even at a male, hockey player-run, machismo boarding school in the 80s. I can think of few women strong enough to walk the path you did. Thank you for walking it! We were so lucky to have you to show us that it's okay to stick up for women, that we are just as important and relevant to society as boys.

Dylan, hiker and outdoor enthusiast who was helpful on the Grand Canyon hike:

Hi Jean,

I love to remember the snow in the canyon, and certainly Gregory's reflective sunglasses and smile.

I laugh as well—the story implies some insecurity at being a leader. It didn't occur to me that any of my teachers would ever have insecurity in this role until I became a teacher myself (a short, two-year tenure between college and graduate school).

Regardless, on this trip you were certainly our leader, and we had more respect for you since you had dealt with your tumor in the previous years. Yet that didn't stop you from leading us. I think our intentions to help you were youthful. Safety, managing the unexpected, innovation, and teamwork were all things we learned in outdoor education, and we were excited to apply them. I remember that we were excited by the challenges: the hike, the desert (snow, yet no water), being able to support our leaders, and succeeding in making the rim. And not just surviving getting to the rim but getting to the rim and feeling proud.

Dana, who called me nearly twenty years after her high school graduation to ask if I thought she should have a baby:

I'm so touched by what you wrote.

I love the quilt you made for my baby. And that you sent me back the letter I wrote you about motherhood? That made me cry.

The thing that went "right" with your relationship is that you're a wonderful person, Jean, and you connect with your students in ways that last a lifetime.

Love,
Dana

Acknowledgments

Many thanks to those who proofread, commented, and spent time with me developing the manuscript. My father, Richard A. Miller, checked the grammar—not only of my high school papers—but this book as well. My other father, Jim Mariner, aided in the initial formats. Many thanks to those who proofread, commented, and spent time with me developing the manuscript. My editor, Melissa Kale, gave valuable suggestions and insights throughout the process.

Meaningful edits and ideas came from those who had heard these stories before, including my adult children—Blaise, EmmaLia, and Liza—and my beloved Paul, who supports me endlessly and tirelessly through all adventures and journeys, including the writing of this memoir.

Reading Group Guide

These sixteen questions are offered as a support for sparking meaningful conversations with friends and colleagues about the topics in *Backward and Blind*. Please feel free to bring your own questions and inspiring ideas to discussions that you facilitate or participate in. To request an author appearance at your event in person or online, email bookclubs@citrinepublishing.com.

1. What are the strongest and most important messages in *Backward and Blind*?

2. What did the title mean to you before reading the book? What does it mean to you now?

3. In what ways did you see your teenage self in any of these stories or did you identify with the teacher—or both?

4. Do these stories inspire you to be a high-school teacher or repel you from assuming this role?

5. Do you believe the skill of teaching can be taught or is it a skill that some people naturally possess? What personality characteristics suit a career in high school teaching? What other skills are important? How would you prioritize the importance of these skills or personality characteristics?

6. The phrase "teaching teens" in the title has a double meaning. What are some examples of how the teens were the teachers?

7. Which stories reflect the greatest learning for the students? Is there a common denominator?

8. How does humor impact the high school classroom? Do you think teachers should integrate or encourage humor into the classroom? How?

9. What are the qualities of an effective teacher? What are the qualities of a deficient teacher? How will the answers to these questions vary?

10. When the author writes, "People are allowed to grow up," what and whom do you think she is talking about?

11. The author taught at a transitional time—when girls started attending a previously all-boys school. Presumably now, awareness is greater and school populations are more welcoming across the board. For example, the notion of "GAFFO" would have shocked any current student or faculty member years ago. The "Me Too" movement has since impacted awareness; notwithstanding, many women have said similar issues have existed in the workplace and still exist today. What progress have you seen in your workplaces and which areas still need greater awareness?

12. Parallels can be made between the gender integration of schools such as the one in this book and desegregation of U.S. schools in the 1960's. Further parallels can be made with the increased awareness and integration of LGBTQ students. What is similar between these transitions and what is different?

13. Compare the author's responses in the two skiing stories—Mark who broke his arm in the introduction and Tammy who had a potential head and neck injury. Other than the potential seriousness of the injury, why do you think the author's response was so different?

14. "Mae" is a young woman who faced traumatic life experiences and was able to overcome them. Why is this an important story?

15. Are you still in contact with any of your adult mentors from your teen years like the author stayed in touch with Mrs. Wilmacar? Why or why not? Are there other mentors with whom you have stayed in contact? If you are a mentor to a young person, what are your plans for staying in touch or not staying in touch?

16. How might the strategies of successfully teaching teenagers be applied to the parenting of teenagers?

About the Author

Raised in New England, Jean A. Miller Mariner moved to Colorado for her first teaching assignment at an independent residential high school. That led to more than thirty years at six different schools teaching middle-school through college-level math and psychology courses, all while rearing three children with her beloved husband. With a Bachelor of Arts from Oberlin and a Master of Arts in Teaching from Colorado College, she also coached swimming, math, and debate competitions; organized community service activities; served as a dorm parent; and wrote for a textbook company. Splitting her time between the mountains of rural Maine and the mountains of the southwest, she identifies as part Southwesterner and part New Englander. Now retired to a wealth of new life experiences, she has revived interests in writing, mountain biking, open water swimming, traveling, fabric arts, and volunteering for a local food bank.

www.JeanAMillerMariner.com

Publisher's Note

Thank you for the opportunity to serve you. If you would like to share this book, here are some popular ways:

REVIEWS
Write an online book review

GIVING
Gift this book to friends, family, and colleagues

BOOK CLUBS
Read it with a group of colleagues or friends

EVENTS
Invite the author to be a speaker for your organization

BULK ORDERS
Email sales@citrinepublishing.com

CONTACT
Call +1-828-585-7030 or email:
info@citrinepublishing.com

We appreciate your book reviews, letters, and shares.

www.ingramcontent.com/pod-product-compliance
Lightning Source LLC
Chambersburg PA
CBHW060523080526
44586CB00012B/590